CELTIC
DEVOTIONAL
DAILY PRAYERS AND BLESSINGS

Celtic Devotional
DAILY PRAYERS AND BLESSINGS

Caitlín Matthews

Harmony Books
New York

For Janet, Iggy and Ignatius Piedilato – may the
blessing of light, love and life surround them and their temenos.

Published by Harmony Books, a division of Crown Publishers, Inc., 201 East 50th Street,
New York, New York 10022. Member of the Crown Publishing Group.

Random House, Inc, New York, Toronto, London, Sydney, Auckland.

HARMONY and colophon are trademarks of Crown Publishers, Inc. Originally published in Great Britain by
Godsfield Press 1996

Printed and bound in Hong Kong.

DESIGNED AND PRODUCED BY THE BRIDGEWATER BOOK COMPANY LTD

Library of Congress Cataloguing-in-Publication Data

Available upon request

ISBN 0-517-70413-7

10 9 8 7 6 5 4 3 2 1

First American Edition

To obtain details of the author's quarterly Hallowquest Newsletter, which gives notice
of her books, tapes, training courses and events, send six first-class stamps (within UK)
or eight international reply paid coupons (outside UK) for a sample copy.

CONTENTS

T HE DIVINE is perceived and experienced in many different ways by individuals and religious groups. Orthodox religions have codified their own approaches to the Divine, defining its inapprehensible mystery in diverse ways. Many people have been helped and encouraged by such approaches, but others have not, feeling that their personal mystical experience cannot be so defined. Whatever the differences of approach, mystics of all persuasions agree that, however we address the Divine, our prayer is heard.

This book is for people of lively, questing spirit who want to lay down a personal pattern of spiritual practice but who do not wish to practice this within a specific religious framework. The material within this book springs from the spiritual current of Celtic tradition, both from the primal, animistic spirituality of early times and from the Celtic Christianity, which was the civilizing influence of Europe. Elements of all parts of the Celtic tradition have been invoked here to create this book.

The primal and Christian streams of Celtic spirituality share one overwhelming characteristic that has made this book possible: their sense of hospitality and welcome. It has been my custom to work and worship with people of many different spiritual backgrounds: this has only been possible when such groups have extended their welcome to me. Without this essential welcome, the soul cannot be at ease. It is for this reason that I have chosen to work within the broadest lines of the Celtic spiritual tradition where no soul is condemned as being beyond salvation, but is treated as integrally holy and full of potential; where no part or inhabitant of the universe is thought of as life- or soul-less, but is honored and respected as a habitation of Divine life.

There are so many difficulties in our daily lives, so few incentives to act responsibly, so little support for personal spiritual growth that it is only within the broadest categories of spiritual hospitality that the soul can be encouraged to find its own natural pathway. This is especially so where the soul has been injured by intolerance and lack of charity, or scandalized by the unholy infighting of formal religion, or by its lack of respect for non-human life-forms and neglect of planetary and universal issues. These and many other reasons may drive people from formal religious

adherence, but they do not stop the need for them to pray, meditate or contemplate in union with the world.

From the beginning of time, people have explored spiritual pathways that have put them into aligned communion with the Divine; it is only latterly that spiritual response has been so severely codified and formalized.

The urge to follow a spiritual pathway comes in a variety of ways, but, in every case, the soul puts out its exploratory shoots in the context of personal devotion, testing the ground, discovering how Spirit responds, learning how true communion with the Divine can be brought about.

"Devotional" comes from the Latin verb, "to devote or dedicate." In common with all devotional aids, this book has been created to help you to dedicate your time in a spiritual way so that your whole life may be consecrated or made holy in the context of your own spiritual experience.

The marking of time by prayer or special periods of devotion is common to all spiritualities. This book is no different, save that it follows the seasonal pattern of the Celtic world. This devotional is divided into five sections: the first four correspond to the Celtic seasonal quarters of the year. The last one contains prayers and blessings for special occasions.

The Celtic seasonal quarters with their Gaelic names are arranged as follows:

SAMHAIN (*pronounced Sow'en*)
November–January, the Winter quarter

IMBOLC (*pronounced Imm'ulk*)
February–April, the Spring quarter

BELTANE (*pronounced Bell'tane*)
May–July, the Summer quarter

LUGHNASADH (*pronounced Loo'nassa*)
August–October, the Autumn quarter

Each season was celebrated in the ancient Irish calendar by a festival marking its opening. In the modern folk calendar, two of these festivals are still celebrated with traditional vigor – Beltane or May-Day, the festival celebrating the return of life, and Samhain or Halloween, that was originally the festival in honor of the ancestors.

The Celtic year may be likened to the life-progress of the soul itself: it starts at the time of cold and darkness and proceeds through the many seasons of life until it reaches fruitful maturity. When we have "made our soul," we pass into the winter of life that our world calls death, but this time with the fruits of our soul thick upon us. Each season provides us with many doorways of opportunity for fresh spiritual revelation and personal response.

When the primal Celtic tribe of the Tuatha de Danaan first established their people in Ireland, Bres, the leader of the former inhabitants of the land, offered them a continual harvest. They refused him, replying,

> *This has been our way:*
> *Spring for plowing and for sowing,*
> *Summer for strengthening the crop,*
> *Autumn for grain's ripeness and for reaping,*
> *Winter for consuming its goodness.*

If we respect the gifts of each season, we will also find the thresholds and doorways of the spirit.

Prayer is not just the preserve of religious people: it is for all. In the primal world traditions, we find prayer attends every act of life. This was also true of the Celtic tradition, which encompassed all aspects of daily life with prayer and invocation. One of the chief characteristics of such prayer was its oral nature, since it was spoken aloud. Among Celtic peoples, the vitality of the truth was preserved by the oral tradition. The educated classes of ancient Celtic society did not write things down, they remembered them. The druids, poets and seers were trained to remember wisdom, history, lore, poetry and story over long years of education. Whatever was spoken had power and primacy.

The very formal attitude to prayer, exemplified by formal religions, is not a natural way to approach the Divine, although there may be special times when the glory and the dancing in our hearts are so great that only words of resonant triumph can express what we feel. At the furthest extreme from formality is an overfamiliar chumminess that hits a discordant note in our soul. If we but remember to keep our prayer oral, we will also preserve its vitality, discovering that prayer and response happen at the level of need and contemporary context.

Prayer is not only about asking, it is about thanking, blessing, praising. Exaggerated forms of worship, adoration and reverence are not currently popular: they are socially acceptable only among the devout in private. However, as everyday mystics, we may personally experience profound spiritual transformations of such potency and fervor that we do indeed understand why the devout dance and sing ecstatically or prostrate themselves in the presence of Divine union, or, like the Celtic poets and saints, pronounce poems or chants of sublime beauty and homage, in total ecstatic identification with the Divine.

Traditional Celtic blessings and spiritual practices are combined here with prayers and meditations specially written for this book. These have arisen from my own devotional practice over many years, inspired and supported by the rich treasury of the Celtic spiritual tradition.

In this book the Divine is addressed by means of a variety of metaphors. Mystics and poets of all eras and spiritualities have called upon the Divine according to the needs of their heart: as rock, door, tree, ground of knowledge; as mother, father, sister, brother, friend, beloved; as keeper, creator, watcher, restorer and giver of hope. Mystics are poets of the spirit who speak with the metaphor of delight. But every living person is also a potential mystic with an immediate and spontaneous response to the wonder of the universe.

We each have our own personal experience of the Divine even though we may have no formal belief. The terms and metaphors by which the Divine is invoked in this devotional are sometimes neutral, sometimes gender-specific: vary these to your own usage, remembering that the Divine is not constrained to either solely male or female forms. Aspects of the Divine, which we might term angels, messengers, spirits or saints, are also invoked: this is not to disrespect or belittle the Divine, but because we all need all the spiritual friends we can find! There are also opportunities to pray to, or ask the help of, any spiritual mentors, teachers and guides whose example has helped us on our path. Mercy, help, love, compassion, guidance also spring from what we have perhaps previously considered as nonanimate or nonensouled sources: from trees, landscapes, animals. There is no thing or being that does not possess its innate spiritual connection with the divine source of the universe. Discover and draw upon the help of whatever attunes your soul to the Divine Spirit.

Find your own place to be centered and still: this may be somewhere inside your house or outside in a garden, park or woods.

Our special place may have more than one use – a quiet kitchen, a semiprivate bedroom or study – but that doesn't make it any less your own hermitage or place of meditation.

Above all, make this book your own in your own ways, in your own words, drawing upon the inspiration of your heart and the needs of your soul. Remember that imagination is the faculty of the soul and that when it suggests new pathways to us we are being invited to explore the territory of the soul in ways that will certainly change and reenchant us.

May you blessedly pass the threshold of the inner country and discover the treasures of the spirit that have always been yours!

Caitlín Matthews
Oxford, England, July 1995

13

HOW TO USE THIS BOOK

ach of the Celtic seasons starts at nightfall with its own invocation whereby its particular gifts and qualities are welcomed into the household in the traditional manner. Similarly, at the close of the season, in the morning, there is a farewell blessing whereby we give thanks for the season that is passing. Each seasonal section has its own beginning and ending invocations, as well as a greeting for the equinox or solstice, which falls midway through the season. Suggested activities for each season are also given.

CHAPTER OPENER

DAILY PRACTICE

Words and images evoke the Celtic gifts of the season in the opening pages of the first four sections.

Key images clearly identify prayers and blessings for days of the week, which are divided into morning and evening practice.

Traditionally, among Celtic countries, the 24-hour duration of a day started at nightfall, time being reckoned in nights and days. Each festival would have had its own communal celebrations. The spirit of each festival is denoted here by a special praise-poem that echoes the traditional "I Am" poems of the great Celtic poets such as Amairgin and Taliesin, who make a mystical identification with the spiritual power of the universe.

Within this book, each of the Celtic seasons has its own week of devotional practices which, because we live in busy times, have been divided into morning and evening practice. Each day of the week has its own variable devotions. Although this devotional week is repeated within each season, each day and night of the solar and lunar month also has its own questions or meditations, and there are also blessings and rituals for special occasions that may be incorporated into daily practice.

Each day has its own solar question and lunar meditation for each day's devotion.

Prayers and blessings for special occasions are illustrated with images from the ancient Celtic world.

The Arrangement of Morning Devotion

MORNING PRACTICE begins with a brief invocation of the Divine, e.g. "Opener of Morning, Source of Recreation. I rise up refreshed this morning." This may be combined with the making of a personal sacred gesture of invitation.

THE SOUL is symbolically "awakened" by an invocation of the primal qualities, e.g. "life, light and love"; this practice corresponds to the traditional awakening of the hearth-fire that takes place in the morning.

EACH DAILY practice has a period of silence: not a dull, unthinking or impatient silence, but a living communion of sacred silence wherein our beings are attuned to the Divine. You are invited to enter into a period of listening silence and deep communion in your period of morning devotion.

You are then invited to call upon your own particular soul-teacher or soul-friends for help and guidance during the day. A soul-teacher is any spiritual luminary, mentor or guide who has shed light upon your path, such as a saint or spiritual exemplar: a soul-teacher is usually someone not now living, although living teachers may be called upon. Soul-friends come in many shapes and sizes: they include our special human friends, animals, places, indeed, anyone or thing with which we share a soul-resonance or spiritual kinship.

TRADITIONALLY, the light of the sun was understood as the spiritual light that illumined the seeker's quest. To this end, a series of questions, one for each calendrical day of the month, is given. There is a time of meditation where you may briefly contemplate and seek the answer to the Solar Question of that day; this section comes at the end of the appropriate seasonal week's devotions. The notion of question and answer is traditionally part of the Celtic learning process where, anciently, knowledge was imparted from mouth to ear: comprehension was subsequently tested by questioning and repetition. The Solar Question of that day may not receive an answer during the time of morning devotion itself, but may spontaneously be resolved later that day or week; some answers may require practical implementation or some prior action to bring them about.

THERE FOLLOWS a series of prayers for specific needs, both group and personal. These may include celebrations, remembrances or blessings. This part of morning devotion may be considerably extended or altered according to the needs of that day.

BEFORE YOU GO out for the day or begin that day's activities, you are invited to make use of that most traditional of Celtic prayer-forms: the protection of the pathway and the soul.

Each season has its own special form: Samhain, *the Breastplate of Wisdom*; Imbolc, *the Encircling of Help*; Beltane, *the Cincture (or Belt) of Protection*; and Lughnasadh, *the Cloak of Covering*.

The taking of soul-protection was a serious business for the Celts, to be performed not solely by the lips but by the motivated mind and the active imagination also. For the Breastplate of Wisdom, imagine the soul-protectors invoked as a shield upon your heart; for the Encircling of Help, see your protectors ringing you lovingly around; for the Cincture of Protection, envisage your protectors circling your waist; for the Cloak of Covering, imagine each protecting quality as a thread in a mantle about your shoulders.

Each form draws upon nine qualities of nine aspects of creation e.g. stars, elements, trees, animals, senses, etc. The Celts of all eras venerated the threefold nature of the universe, whether of Mother, Father, Child or of Heaven, Earth and Sea. The protective power of that threefold nature when multiplied by itself to make nine is the most commonly recurrent theme of Celtic prayer-forms.

MORNING PRACTICE ends with a blessing and may be combined with personal sacred gestures signifying the end of your devotion.

The Arrangement of Evening Devotion

EVENING DEVOTION starts with a brief invocation of the Divine, recalling you to your sacred practice. It may be combined with a personal sacred gesture of invitation.

YOU MAY choose to light a candle at the fall of dark to accompany each of the candle-prayers that start evening devotion: the candle may be extinguished at the end of your practice or may be left to burn safely upon your own domestic shrine.

EVENING DEVOTION has its patterns of clarifying what the day has brought. Seeking a spiritual expression can be a means of ego-enhancement and self-seeking, where we become so entrenched in our personal growth that we ignore the rest of the world. You are encouraged to go beyond the confines of the ego by means of regular self-clarification whereby the personal daily life is scrutinized and put into the greater perspective of the universe.

Self-clarification is a daily process wherein we shift through the day's "stuff" and neutrally consider how it is to be understood, what experiences have been useful or beneficial, which are painful or embarrassing; then, without guilt or self-blame, lay into our soul's treasury what has helped us and offer for transformation that which burdens us. This process calls upon the soul-teacher and soul-friends to give transformative help and insights that will help us make the necessary changes.

You are invited to enter into communion with the Divine and seek the living silence once more.

THE TWIN lights of sun and moon track morning and evening devotion. While the morning is challenged by a question that puts our souls on their mettle, in the evening we allow a space of reflective tranquillity wherein we meditate discursively upon the Lunar Meditation, taken from the end section of the appropriate season. The light of the moon traditionally corresponds to the mystery of the Divine; each meditation subject is brought into the space of the soul and allowed to develop and reveal itself in its own manner. Responses to both the Solar Question and the Lunar Meditation can be briefly recorded in a journal along with dreams, visions, hopes and desires. To determine the lunar phase accurately, a Perpetual Lunar Calendar can be found on p.116.

 THERE FOLLOWS a sequence of prayers for specific needs, both group and personal.

HAVING AWAKENED the soul in the morning, you now bring it to a point of stillness and rest, in readiness for sleep. The blessing of the soul is extended to all beings.

EVENING DEVOTION ends with an invocation to the Divine. Again, this can be combined with a personal sacred gesture of peace.

The prayers, meditations, practices and patterns outlined in this devotional are not to be followed slavishly; at every turn you are invited to draw forth expressions of your own devising, from your own need. If there is anything here that jars against your personal taste, please feel free to ignore it and substitute something more suitable of your own. This is a book that needs its own inhabitant soul to create in a practical way personal and comfortable space within it, so that you may be able to accept the spiritual hospitality that is most welcome to you.

This book has been written to be used by anyone in any country; if you live in the Southern Hemisphere, then it is sensible to mark the seasons by the following dates:

Samhain, Season of Winter *1 May–31 July*
Winter Solstice 21 June
Imbolc, Season of Spring *1 August–31 October*
Spring Equinox 21 September
Beltane, Season of Summer *1 November–31 January*
Summer Solstice 21 December
Lughnasadh, Season of Autumn *1 February–30 April*
Autumn Equinox 21 March

SAMHAIN

THE WINTER *quarter of Samhain brings the gifts of restoration and renewal, as the cold weather closes in, so the soul is led to more reflective depths. It is traditionally associated with the remembrance of the ancestors, with the coming of death and the conception of new life. In the human growth cycle, Samhain corresponds to the period of old age when wisdom, freedom of spirit and clarity are experienced. Samhain is a good time to celebrate the lives of all wise elders, all those whose actions and ideas have brought resolution and peace, all holy ones whose sacrifice have brought new life and opened spiritual thresholds to all.*

FOR THE WEEKS BETWEEN
1 NOVEMBER AND 31 JANUARY

Greetings and Farewells during Samhain

SONG OF SAMHAIN

I am the hallow-tide of all souls passing,
  I am the bright releaser of all pain,
I am the quickener of the fallen seed-case,
  I am the glance of snow, the strike of rain.
I am the hollow of the winter twilight,
  I am the hearth-fire and the welcome bread,
I am the curtained awning of the pillow,
  I am unending wisdom's golden thread.

THRESHOLD INVOCATION
FOR THE FESTIVAL OF SAMHAIN

(to be said at the front door of the house on the
eve of Samhain, 31 October, in the evening)

Grandmother Wisdom, open the door,
  Grandfather Counsel, come you in.
Let there be welcome to the ancient lore,
  Let there be welcome to the Winter of the Year.
In cold and darkness you are traveling,
  Under crystal skies you will arrive.
May the blessed time of Samhain
  Clarify the soul of all beings,
Bringing joy and wisdom to revelation.
  From the depths to the heights,
From the heights to the depths,
  In the cave of every soul.

GREETING TO THE WINTER SOLSTICE
(21 December)

Brightener of Darkness, hail!
  Keeper of Clearness, Opener of
the Depths.
  Gifts of plenty are arising,
Winter wonders, white snows' fall.
Joyful be the heart within us,
  Open wide the guesting door,
Wisdom waken in abundance,
  Warm our beings to the core.

FAREWELL TO THE SEASON OF SAMHAIN

(to be said at the back door/window of the
house on the last morning of the Samhain
quarter, 31 January)

Go with thanks and go with blessing,
  Season of deep memory.
Souls with joy are deeply freighted,
  Hearts are charged with heritage.
As ancestors you have traveled,
  You have come to Winter's home.
Father Counsel, who has cheered us,
  Mother Wisdom, who has smiled,
Touch the hidden seed within us,
  May we grow as Spring's own child.

23

Activities for the Winter Months

PRACTICE *introspection, meditation, contemplation*, drawing upon the peaceful sanctuary of this season.

❄

SHIFT *burdens* by doing something about them (e.g. make your will) or by giving up unnecessary patterns.

❄

REMEMBER your *ancestors* and *celebrate* their wisdom.

❄

IN THIS deep season of darkness and introspection, *seek the sun* at midnight, the rich treasures that lie in the lap of Winter.

❄

BE AWARE of the *ancestral teachers*, the grandparents and elders of the spiritual traditions, whose footsteps have kept the pathways open.

CUT *back old growth* in the garden
and burn or compost it. Dig over the soil
in preparation for the Spring.

✼

WALK and *meditate* outdoors for
at least ten minutes daily.

✼

IDENTIFY *the nature* of the soil and rock-
forms in your locality and how this affects
the life-forms who live upon the land.

✼

BE ACTIVE, with like-minded others, in
recording, preserving, living and *learning
about* the ancient wisdom of indigenous
peoples, especially those in your own land.

✼

AS YOU travel through the land of
Winter, relate your *spiritual journey* to the
wisdom of this season.

MONDAY
morning

Grandfather of Vision,
Grandmother of Waking Memory,
I dedicate this waking to you.

I sing the hearth-song of my soul,
note of love,
note of light,
note of life,
attune the music of my
winter-wakening soul.
Preserve my soul in wisdom:
may it sing forth with the clearness of
the winter sun.

Wealth of the World, whose bounty is never spent, I come in quietness to the treasury of silence ~ SACRED SILENCE ~ I give thanks for the nurture and blessing that you leave within my soul.

O many-gifted teacher of my soul, as the Winter world awakens, so I stretch out my hands for your companionship this day that I may understand the questions of this day ~ SOLAR QUESTION.

For the great variety of spiritual expression and for spiritual freedom, I give loving thanks. I call upon the Encompasser of Souls to breathe light and liberation into those places where spiritual self-determination is constrained or is punished.

May the great work of science be guided by the Source of all Mystery in wise and considerate ways: may no soul be harmed, may no living being suffer torment or be treated without respect in the inquiries and researches of science.

Wise-men, Wise-women, Holy Ones of all generations I call to you to send a blessing upon all who are stuck in the past and walk the spirals of an inturning maze: may your wisdom lead them by fresh and fruitful pathways to the blessing of the present moment.

I don the breastplate of wisdom:
wisdom of star,
courtesy of spirit,
endurance of wind,
strength of warrior,
honor of maiden,
poetry of lover,
beauty of flower,
nobility of animal,
silence of earth.
Nine wisdoms guarding my heart
this day without fear.

Ancient and Enduring One,
Keeper of Kindreds,
I go forth as one of your family.

26

MONDAY
e v e n i n g

Gate of Gladness,
Door of Joy,
I cross your threshold this Winter's night.

Twilight, dark night, deep night sounding,
freight of soul to swell-note rounding,
spark of light shall bring to grounding.

As the winter stars appear in the darkness of the heavens, I call upon my soul's teacher to show to me the sources of hope that have been revealed today ~ SELF-CLARIFICATION ~ May the stars witness the renewal of hope in the darkest night.

Weaver of Wonder, you have stretched the net of the heavens to catch a school of stars; I celebrate the network of the universe and silently wonder at my own part within it ~ SACRED SILENCE ~ I give thanks that within your tapestry I am safely woven; grant me understanding of your bright mystery ~ LUNAR MEDITATION.

I give thanks to the wise powers of the universe that have protected me this day: may their blessing attend me wherever I go.

Many are in transition, awaiting rehabilitation, training for new livelihoods, biding between new home and old, biding between life and death, or between unbecoming and birth: Traveler of the Galaxy, be their companion as they wait this night.

For all who have forgotten the joy of the spiritual path, I ask a blessing: may the Holy Ones bestow memory of spiritual sweetness and deliverance from stale observances.

I bring to mind all who have touched my life today and who are in need . . . .

I tune the hearth-song of my soul,
loving words upon my lips,
light-giving songs upon my heart,
life-bringing praises upon my eyes.
The music of comfort resound in the
souls of all beings,
preserving them in peace
as the sun and moon renew themselves
this night.

With the Star-Kindler
and the Guardian of Planets,
I pass into the blessed darkness;
of one being with the stars,
of one motion with the galaxy.

TUESDAY
m o r n i n g

Mother of Memory,
Father of the Dream,
I rise from the embrace of sleep
to the miracle of morning.

I waken my soul at the harp of harmony:
chord of grace, chord of gladness,
chord of glory,
beautify my being, awaken my heart, inspire
my soul.
The chorus of peace preserve my soul
this day of hard Winter.

Weaver of Life, Receiver of Death, you teach us time and eternity and the blessing of change. In the silence of our meeting, reveal to me how I also need to change ~ SACRED SILENCE ~ Your merciful compassion is my guide.

Soul-friends, teacher of my soul, your revolutionary influence upon me shows me the curve of my life's spiral. May I be ever true to the spiritual pathway as it reveals itself every day. Help me to meditate upon the question of this day ~ SOLAR MEDITATION.

I remember all in the realms of light, the dear ones and Holy Ones whose vocation is a template for my own, whose life-ways have opened my own pathway, especially . . . . May they enjoy concord, joy and felicity.

On all who are prevented from gaining an education through poverty, location, sex or social class, I ask a blessing: may the Holy Ones bestow upon them an inquiring intelligence and the means to learn and to understand.

For all who are entering retirement and those who have lost their employment: may the creative renewal of this space of time unfold fresh possibilities of life and of livelihood.

I don the breastplate of wisdom:
wrought of the nine metals:
strength of iron,
smoothness of silver,
servicableness of tin,
beauty of copper,
truth of gold,
endurance of platinum,
brightness of bronze,
glow of brass,
shield of lead.
Wise metals of earth's own heart,
cover my breast, protect my soul,
this Winter's day,
till Winter's night.

The blessing of the Mirror of Mercy,
the Crystal of Revelation,
accompany me this day;
may I be your true likeness
in the wanderings of the world.

TUESDAY
e v e n i n g

Wealth of the World,
Ransomer of Souls,
I return through your mercy this
Winter's night.

Winter stillness, shadows falling,
Waxen light brings day to wane;
Gift of rest and mercy's calling,
Ending hurt and spirit's pain.

As the day falls into darkness, I ask my soul's teacher to help me recognize what is finished, not to manipulate the powers of life and death to keep alive what is really worn out this day ~ SELF-CLARIFICATION ~ May all the out-worn things that I have harbored find their true rest and eternal home.

Lady of Assemblies, Chieftain of Tribes, I am gathered to your sacred meeting place this Winter evening to hear the council of your peace ~ SACRED SILENCE ~ May this glad gathering give me strength to follow your council, and to track your mystery with obedience ~ LUNAR MEDITATION.

I ask a blessing upon all women who no longer menstruate: may the Wise Grandmothers, the Holy Ones of all Ages, bestow upon them the serenity and fulfillment of their wisdom.

Lady of Animals, Lord of Beasts, your creatures harbor no bitterness in them: protect and relieve from pain all creatures who are trapped or imprisoned at this time. May human animals learn respect for all their animal kindred.

I give thanks for the powers of the metals that have been my breastplate this day: may we respect the bounty of the earth, may we not mar her fair face with pollution and devastation.

Teacher of Tribes, you know the needs of my own family, especially . . . . May your trust and love fill the hearts of all whom I love.

I soothe my soul with the harp of harmony:
chord of beauty grace my being,
chord of repose gladden my heart,
chord of inspiration glorify my soul.
May the chorus of peace
resound in the souls of all beings
this chill Winter's night.

Grandfather of Day's End,
Grandmother of the Deep Darkness,
Into your deep hill I am gathered for my
Winter's sleep.

WEDNESDAY
morning

Grandmother of the Living Light,
Grandfather of the Day's Birth
Out of your hill of sleep I rise refreshed.

I kindle my soul at the hearth-fires of Winter,
warmth of welcome,
warmth of working,
warmth of nurture,
be upon my lips, my hands, my being,
this Winter day
till Winter's night.

Holy Grandparents of the Universe, you have watched the world from its birth, through many ages, I seek your silence that I also may grow in wisdom ~ SACRED SILENCE ~ I celebrate the vision of your enduring life in me.

Counselor of my soul, you quicken my soul's progress this Winter day by the strength of your example. I look to your light to help me discover the track of this day's question ~ SOLAR MEDITATION.

I celebrate the wild and untamed places of the planet: Keeper of the Wilderness, keep yet the untrammeled wildness of the world in which we live, keep it for your own glory.

I look to the unfulfilled places in my life: may the Holy Ones show me how best to prepare these as fields where I may sow seeds of hope, especially . . . .

May a blessing be granted to all who are unemployed: may self-blame, disappointment and the sense of uselessness be transformed by self-confidence, hopefulness and a sense of potential.

I don the breastplate of wisdom,
wrought of the nine jewels of the heart:
dew of faery women,
spear of faery hosts,
blood of ravens,
wilderness of eagle,
ocean of seagulls,
music of poets,
love of lovers,
children of mothers,
wisdom of souls.
Nine radiant jewels to cover my heart,
to protect my soul this Winter day,
this Winter night.

May the blessing of the
Guardian of the Hallow-tide,
the Keeper of Winter's Hearth,
attend me this day as I go forth.

WEDNESDAY
e v e n i n g

Door of Welcome,
Keeper of Good Cheer,
I come home on the Hallow-tide,
under the chill of Winter's breath,
to the warmth of the hearth.

Seed-flame quickening,
Winter's store,
riches hidden in earth's maw,
star-seed flickering, hearts alight,
now conceive the soul's hearth light.

As I withdraw from the day's business like a hermit seeking the solace of peace, so I call upon my soul's teacher to help me see the inner truth of this day's events ~ SELF-CLARIFICATION ~ May the lantern of the truthful light shine in all dark places.

Grandmother Wisdom, Grandfather Understanding, your infinite mercy has held me in loving trust this day, as night deepens, imbue me with perfect stillness and attention as I listen to you ~ SACRED SILENCE ~ Your presence bestows the gift of Winter's insight. I ask your help to show to me the mystery of this night ~ LUNAR MEDITATION.

I remember all who cannot ask for help through pride or because they do not know that help is near,

and in this space I lend my prayers, especially to . . . .

Teacher of the Universe, there is no time in life when I cease from learning: please help me to see where I need to be more receptive to the lessons of experience, that I may be prepared for the path ahead of me . . .

I ask a blessing upon all who are outcast by society: upon those suffering from immune-system diseases, upon the homeless, upon the graceless and ugly, upon all mentally disturbed people who have been set adrift in the world; may the Holy Ones protect and support them all and lead them to hearths of welcome.

For the nine jewels of the heart that have been my breastplate this day, I give thanks: may the desires of my own heart be acknowledged, especially . . . .

I gather my soul at the hearth-fires of Winter,
warmth of welcome upon my lips,
warmth of rest upon my hands,
warmth of nurture upon my being.
May the souls of all beings
be wrapped in the warmth of peace
this Winter's night
till Winter's dawning.

Keeper of the Cosmos,
Kindler of Starlight,
Bringer of Sleep,
I rest with you this night.

31

✷

THURSDAY
m o r n i n g

Diviner of the Mystery,
Catalyst of Creation,
I rise up with you.

◎

I bathe my soul in the well of wisdom:
drop of protection,
drop of strength,
drop of healing,
be upon my being, my mind, my heart.
May the triple blessing be upon my soul
from dawn's chill light,
till swift twilight.

Piercer of Doubt, Kindler of Hope, some mornings I am slow to quicken to the pulse of life. Whatever my state of being may I never be slow to turn to you and seek the cell of silence ~ SACRED SILENCE ~ My heart is a kything place where we ever meet.

Soul-friends all, teacher of my soul, please show me the steady ways to hold my spiritual path with confidence; show me the daily practices that lead to perfect skill and alignment ~ SOLAR MEDITATION.

I give thanks for the golden links of lore that our ancestors remembered and that spill into our hands: for the treasures of tradition, for the rich heritage of wisdom, for the ancestral experience that I inherit in every cell of my body.

Somewhere in the world this day wars and conflicts are brewing or already in progress; may all the souls of all beings who suffer the oppression of war – people, animals, plants and places – be guarded and protected by the Holy Ones, and may peace prevail again.

Reconciler and Healer of Hearts, I ask your blessing upon the children, women and men who are involved in the painful process of divorce; may the love that can endure such separation be brightened and the hatred that separation can cause be diminished.

I don the breastplate of wisdom:
protection of evergreens guard my heart,
brightness of pine,
sharpness of holly,
protection of juniper,
courage of laurel,
nobility of cypress,
endurance of yew,
health of eucalyptus,
splendor of cedar,
beauty of arbutus.
Nine evergreens to guard my breast
this Winter day,
this Winter night.

May the blessing of the True Taker
and the Glad Giver be upon me
as I brave the winds of Winter.

THURSDAY
e v e n i n g

Into the arms of the Bright Surrender,
Into the lap of Lovely Peace,
I make my way and take my refuge.

Candle flickers, day's end,
Winter shivers, night's friend;
brightness echoes heart's giving,
soul's quickness ever-living.

As the Winter closes about our ears and the wind blows chill, I call upon my soul's teacher to show me the progress of the day ~ SELF-CLARIFICATION ~ In the depths of doubt and uncertainty, may we be always shown the next step of the road.

Teller of Tales, you have sung the story of the universe as one great web of wonder. In wondering silence now I enter the heart of our story ~ SACRED SILENCE ~ I give thanks for the privilege of being part of this unfolding tale. Please help me read the radiant revelation of your Winter mystery in the dark heavens ~ LUNAR MEDITATION.

I recall the lost opportunities of this year which I have failed to grasp ... ; Keeper of Thresholds, I thank you for your trust in me and ask from your hands the gifts of timeliness and confidence to step across the doorsill of fresh opportunity.

Holy Ones of all ages, comfort those who are without comfort this night, give ease to troubled hearts, restore hope to those that are hopeless and give them the lasting blessing of peace.

As Winter deepens and daylight lessens, I call upon the Spinner of the Seasons to bring the illumination of Samhain's gift to all souls, especially to . . . . May the icy winds and the bright snows of Winter bring space and clarity to all who are heavy-burdened.

I give thanks for the wise qualities of the evergreen trees that have stood by me this day: may you show me how my own heart can be evergreen and growing through winters of doubt and darkness.

I cleanse my soul in the well of wisdom:
protection of being,
strength of mind,
healing of heart,
be the triple cleansing of wisdom.
May the blessing-drop be upon all beings,
conferring wisdom from swift twilight
till dawn's chill light.

The blessing of the Eagle-winged Renewer,
the blessing of the Raven-winged Transformer,
attend my soul this Winter's night.
May all that burdens my being
be lifted as I mount on wings of
dreams this night.

33

✸

FRIDAY
m o r n i n g

From the Wakener of Purpose,
From the Caller of Compassion,
I take my song this Winter morning.

◎

I clarify my soul in the snows of Winter:
crystal of truth,
crystal of nature,
crystal of knowledge,
clarify any darkness
in my breast, my being, my mind.
Three candles to cleanse my soul
from broad daylight
till dim of night.

Everlasting One, you create and renew whatever you will; I ask you to recreate and renew me in the clasp of your closeness ~ SACRED SILENCE ~ In the peace of your silence I am rewoven.

Teacher of my soul, when I am wrapped in gloom, bring me the lightness of humor by whatever means you will. Teach me surrender to the clear call of freedom in laughter's gift and show me the joy in curious questioning ~ SOLAR MEDITATION.

Gatherer and Healer of Souls, may you be first to the site of any disaster to lead souls to peace and to heal anguish; may your Holy Ones direct and guide all rescuers to recover all who are living yet lost.

I ask a blessing on all facing old age, with its unfamiliar infirmities, loneliness and isolation: may the Wise Ones, holy in all ages, bestow the living light of healing, solace, companionship upon them.

As the deep treasury of Winter opens its door, I look into my heart to see which personal gifts and talents I have been hoarding . . . . May I treasure these precious gifts by the holy use of action and practice.

〈〈〈〈〈

I don the breastplate of wisdom,
wrought of the constellations of Winter:
vigilance of Orion,
splendor of Taurus,
flow of Eridanus,
cunning of Perseus,
focus of Ursa Major,
speed of Auriga,
loyalty of Canis Major,
faithfulness of Gemini,
patience of Cassiopeia.
Nine star-powers upon my breast
to preserve my soul,
from crack of light
till fall of night.

♱

Cunning Woman,
Trickster and Clown,
keep me street-wise
to the wiles of the world
this Winter day till I come home to you.

34

FRIDAY
e v e n i n g

Anchor of Ages,
Barque of Bliss,
I sail home upon the homing tides
of Winter.

Winter wakens, earth is shaken,
starlight kindles in the dark;
may the chill heart, unforsaken,
brighten at this warm soul's spark.

Soul-friends all, you have companioned me this long day; with the help of my soul-teacher, give me grace to review its events without blame or guilt ~ *SELF-CLARIFICATION* ~ I thank you for your clarity and compassion.

Keeper of the Soul's Door, you make me a steward of your treasury, a guardian of your gates whenever you lead me into the silence of prayer ~ *SACRED SILENCE* ~ May I be always worthy to open my heart's door to you. Now, as Winter draws deeper, I look up to the heavens to understand your mystery ~ *LUNAR MEDITATION.*

I celebrate the splendor of serendipity, the coincidence of Spirit that reveals the underside of life's tapestry: may I never fall into forgetfulness that what is woven on my side of the cosmic web is but one reality of a great reality. May the shadow-dance of Divine Wisdom ever lighten my life.

May all who have been defeated and conquered receive a blessing: may the Holy Ones help restore to them the garment of self-respect, bestowing the blessing of daily routine and the return of good order.

Security of finances, of livelihood, of dwelling perturb my mind and drive sleep away: Ever-present Provider, I bring my needs to you . . . .

I give thanks to the brilliant constellations of Winter that have glittered on my breast this day.

I veil my soul in the blessing of Winter:
blessing of truth on my breast,
blessing of nature about my being,
blessing of knowledge in my mind.
The blessing of peace upon all beings,
this night and every night,
this season and every season.
Three candles to bless my soul
from broad daylight
till dim of night.

On the Ship of Silence I am safely borne
to the Shore of Wonder;
this Winter's night I seek the harbor of sleep.

SATURDAY
m o r n i n g

PRACTICE FOR EACH SATURDAY IN SAMHAIN

Sustainer of Life,
Eternally Wise One,
From the shrine of sleep I rise up.

I sain* my soul with the
three drops of the cauldron:
dew of originality,
dew of inspiration,
dew of imagination,
make holy my soul, my heart, my mind,
within the soul-shrine of my body.
May my soul be preserved
from chill dawn's light
till swift twilight.

Glad Giver, True Taker, as the raven stoops upon decay and cleanses the earth, so also do you take to yourself all scattered beings, keeping safe their souls. In the mercy of your silence I stand between life and death ~ SACRED SILENCE ~ May the life blood in my veins bring me to perfect mindfulness of my soul's purpose.

Soul-friends and teachers, you are my companions in the game of life. Keep my heart playful and daring by the skill and inspiration of your craft and help me to consider the issue of this day ~ SOLAR MEDITATION.

*Sain means to make holy

I ask a blessing on all who have become separated from those they love, from activities that give them refreshment, from soul-nurture that they deeply need: may the Holy Ones grant release from these self-imposed boundaries that separate the soul from its true nourishment.

As the Winter deepens, it calls us to celebrate the fallowness of the growing seasons and to respect our own fallow times as periods of rest and reflection: I look to my own life and see where I need to be obedient to Winter's stillness . . . .

I don the breastplate of wisdom:
wrought of the nine choice gems:
strength of diamond,
richness of ruby,
holiness of pearl,
protection of amethyst,
counsel of jasper,
mystery of opal,
welcome of garnet,
healing of emerald,
clarity of sapphire.
Nine gems to sparkle and protect my soul
this Winter's day till Winter's night.

Singer of Soul-Song,
Harper of Planet's Harmony,
I dance this day with you.

SATURDAY
e v e n i n g

Singer of Heart's Peace,
Harper of Soul's Desire,
I run home on wings of song.

Winter wakens icy gleam,
Candles sparkle in the stream,
Open now my soul's dream.

This glad day, I seek you out, soul-friends and teachers all to celebrate and rejoice this Winter day: show me how to come to the heart of Winter's joy ~ SELF-CLARIFICATION.

Glad Giver, True Taker, you hold the threads of life within your hands; both the greatest and the smallest creature is in your care; as I enter the cave of your silence I come to the source of life ~ SACRED SILENCE ~ In the cave of silence I am remade, as the day is reborn of the night; reveal to me the beauty of your revelation ~ LUNAR MEDITATION.

Into the hands of the Grandparents of Life and Death I commit the souls of all who have passed from this life: may they find peace, clarity and restoration.

I give thanks to the wise qualities of the nine gems that have been my breast-plate this day: may I always remember that though life forms seem inanimate they do not lack spirit.

I consider the moment of my own death: may I be wellprepared and worthy to enter the Land of the Living.

May my life be lived with virtue and integrity, may my soul-friends help me prepare for my death, however unlikely it now seems, that my dear ones are not weighted down with cares and responsibilities that I could have spared them. I make a frank appraisal of the things that I have left undone that must be completed before I die . . . .

I seal my soul with the
three drops of the cauldron:
originality of soul,
inspiration of heart,
imagination of mind
make holy my being,
in the soul-shrine of my body.
May all souls be preserved in peace
from swift twilight
till chill dawn's light.

Renewer of Worlds,
Transformer of Galaxies,
into your shrine of sleep I sink down,
without fear, without care, without sorrow,
to be remade in you.

SUNDAY
m o r n i n g

Ageless and Unchanging Wisdom,
Mystic and Encompassing Counsel,
I rise up on eagle's wings with you.

I waken my soul at the harp of poets:
string of joy,
string of peace,
string of truth,
resound in my heart, my soul, my mouth.
May my soul be preserved in harmony
from Winter's day
till Winter's night.

Grandmother Wisdom, Grandfather Counsel, you have steered my soul through the shoals of dreams this night, bring me now into the harbor of your peace ~ SACRED SILENCE ~ I give thanks to you for showing me the landmarks of my soul's shore.

Wise teachers and soul-friends of my Winter's pilgrimage, I seek to arrive in safety; please assist and inspire· me through the dark Winter days, as I go on my pilgrim way, seeking the answers that my soul needs ~ SOLAR MEDITATION.

I ask a blessing on the many native peoples whose ancestral heritage is threatened: may the Holy Ancestors and the Holy Messengers of the Divine work together to preserve and transmit the sacred regalia of tradition for the descendants of earth's people.

I give thanks for all who have answered the Caller of Souls to fulfill their spiritual vocation in selfless ways, whether within religions, in charities or in the wide spectrum of the world's work, especially . . . . May those who have set aside their own comfort to comfort others be blessed.

In the chill depths of Winter, I remember all who have grown cold in their affections, who have lost love: may the Holy Ones bring them to the life-fires of the Universal Heart, there to rekindle their hearts.

I don the breastplate of wisdom,
the nine jewels of the gifted ones:
song of poetry,
sustenance of reflection,
strength of meditation,
deepening of lore,
response of research,
replenishment of knowledge,
illumination of intelligence,
nurture of understanding,
exaltation of wisdom.
The nine jewels of bards and druids
shield and protect my soul
from scathe this Winter day.

Sustainer of Life, Giver of Death,
may I be held in your blessed balance
this Winter's day.

SUNDAY
e v e n i n g

Harmony of Heaven,
Resonance of Earth,
I return with you.

Winter stars have lent their brightness
To this candle in the dark;
May my heart be ever questing
For the source of spirit's spark.

With the eternal eyes of my soul's teacher, I look back upon this week and appreciate in what ways I have been part of the history of the planet ~ SELF-CLARIFICATION ~ May the testimony of this week shine out in the annals of time.

Turner of Seasons, it is your design that the dark days of Winter shall be followed by the resurrection of Spring; as my heart grows wintry, may your true clarity germinate whatever will be born in me next season ~ SACRED SILENCE ~ In your loving pattern I am quickened and conceived; as the long night looks for morning, so do I look to your mystery ~ LUNAR MEDITATION.

I give thanks to the nine jewels of the gifted ones; may we respect the teachings and traditions of our ancestors, which bring us inspiration, strength, wisdom and compassion.

All over the planet social reformers and ecological practitioners are striving to bring better balance to all living beings; may the Holy Ones bless their work and lead more beings to implement and support it, especially in the areas of . . . .

I celebrate the moments of well-being that irrigate my life, especially when . . . . I give thanks for these small but precious gifts that bring sanity to the chaos and business of daily life.

For all souls who are conceived this night, I ask a blessing: may the Keeper of Souls send them surely down the star-paths to their mother's wombs and strengthen those parents who lack trust in their abilities to parent.

I soothe my soul at the harp of poets:
joy of heart,
peace of soul,
truth of utterance,
resound in living light this evening.
May the soul of all beings be preserved in
harmony
from Winter's night
till Winter's day.

Grandmother of Memory,
Grandfather of the Dream,
May I sleep safely in you.

39

Solar Questions for Samhain

These questions are part of the morning devotion, to be asked and answered during that time, or to be considered during the day. Some of the answers may reveal aspects of yourself you had not considered, some may require practical implementation. Each day corresponds to the calendrical date, for example: on 2 December, you consult the question on Day 2 below.

~ 1 ~
What are you attempting to manifest now?

~ 2 ~
Do you appreciate the other side of the argument?

~ 3 ~
What do you most hope for?

~ 4 ~
Where do you need to exercise self-control?

~ 5 ~
What is the source of your creativity?

~ 6 ~
Are you neglecting sources of soul-nurture?

~ 7 ~
Which of your plans needs better motivation?

~ 8 ~
What are you homesick for?

~ 9 ~
What skills need to come into play in your life?

~ 10 ~
In which areas do you most need to grow?

~ 11 ~
Which old desires do you need to relinquish?

~ 12 ~
Where is the wool being pulled over your eyes?

~ 13 ~
What is the source of your inspiration?

~ 14 ~
How are you respecting or abusing friendship?

~ 15 ~
Where are you most vulnerable?

~ 16 ~
What is seeking to reveal itself in your dreams?

~ 17 ~
Are you fulfilling your spiritual vocation?

~ 18 ~
What obstructions need to be cleared from your life?

~ 19 ~
What prejudices are you holding on to?

~ 20 ~
What is the source of your spiritual guidance?

~ 21 ~
What do you most appreciate about being human?

~ 22 ~
What do you need to learn in order to be more confident?

~ 23 ~
What is the source of your deepest refreshment?

~ 24 ~
Which of your family do you most appreciate?

~ 25 ~
To whom do you need to show more sensitivity?

~ 26 ~
What would give your loved ones most pleasure?

~ 27 ~
What new idea is seeding itself within you this Winter?

~ 28 ~
What threshold of attainment waits for you to cross over?

~ 29 ~
Which fear is keeping you in prison?

~ 30 ~
What are the landmarks of your spiritual home?

~ 31 ~
What does the seasonal cycle of renewal offer you?

Lunar Meditations for Samhain

The following meditation subjects may be selected for the appropriate phase of the moon each evening: check the Perpetual Moon Calendar on p.116 for the appropriate phase of the moon.

~ 1 ~
The gifts of mortality.

~ 2 ~
Memory of childhood winters.

~ 3 ~
Service to the universe.

~ 4 ~
The wonder of life.

~ 5 ~
Thresholds of light in your life.

~ 6 ~
Music of your choice.

~ 7 ~
The courage to fail and try again.

~ 8 ~
The potency of dreams enacted.

~ 9 ~
The work of your hands.

~ 10 ~
The blessings of age.

~ 11 ~
The unfolding vision of your life.

~ 12 ~
The ancestral memories of your body.

~ 13 ~
Your kinship with the stars.

~ 14 ~
The unconquerable nature of the soul.

~ 15 ~
The treasures of Winter.

~ 16 ~
The cordial of praise.

~ 17 ~
The message of the wind.

~ 18 ~
The satisfaction of conclusion.

~ 19 ~
The truth of the imagination.

~ 20 ~
The constellation that your soul-friends make.

~ 21 ~
The spirit of the land in Winter.

~ 22 ~
The joy of simplicity.

~ 23 ~
The dormant life of the seed.

~ 24 ~
Journey's end.

~ 25 ~
The life made available by decay.

~ 26 ~
The magic of snow.

~ 27 ~
The wandering path of the soul.

~ 28 ~
Memory of dear ones dead or absent.

~ 29 ~
The legacy of wisdom you would bequeath to your descendants.

IMBOLC

THE SPRING quarter of Imbolc brings the gift of insight and inspiration and is a time of beginnings and of essential truthfulness. Begun in the dark and often icy days of early Spring, it is traditionally the time to appreciate innocence, truth and justice, to make resolutions and plans and to prepare for the enfolding year. In the human growth cycle, Imbolc corresponds to the period of childhood when all things are questioned or enjoyed for their own sake. Imbolc is a good time to celebrate the lives of all "soul-mid-wives" who have taught and prepared us, all who have been upholders of justice and truth, all holy ones who have gone to the heart of the matter with great clarity and insight.

FOR THE WEEKS BETWEEN
1 FEBRUARY AND 30 APRIL

Greetings and Farewells during Imbolc

SONG OF IMBOLC

I am the unopened bud, and I the blossom,
I am the lifeforce gathering to a crest,
I am the still companion of the silence,
I am the farflung seeker of the quest.
I am the daughter gathering in wisdom,
I am the son whose questions never cease,
I am the dawn-light searching out glad justice,
I am the center where all souls find peace.

THRESHOLD INVOCATION FOR THE FESTIVAL OF IMBOLC

(to be said at the front door of the house on the eve of Imbolc, 31 January, in the evening)

Midwife of Mystery, open the door,
Infant of the Infinite, come you in.
Let there be welcome to the newborn truth,
Let there be welcome to the Spring of the Year.
In cold and darkness you are traveling,
In warmth and brightness you will arrive.
May the blessed time of Imbolc
Kindle the soul of all beings,
Bringing birth to innocence and integrity
From the depths to the heights,
From the heights to the depths,
In the heart of every soul.

GREETING TO THE SPRING EQUINOX (21 March)

Glad Bringer of Brightness, hail!
  Maiden of Grace, Lad of Laughter.
Gifts of vigor are returning,
  Spring's surprise, rainbow's embrace.
Quickened be the heart within us,
  Opened be our souls to grace,
May the blessing be abiding,
  Welcome sit in every face.

FAREWELL TO THE SEASON OF IMBOLC

(to be said at the back door/window of the house on
the last morning of Imbolc, 30 April)

Go with thanks and go with blessing,
  Season of integrity.
Souls with truth are deeply freighted
  Hearts are keen with innocence.
In the cold and darkness traveling,
  You have come to brightest Spring.
Infant, who has grown to childhood,
  Midwife, wise with mothering,
Touch the hidden beauty in us,
  Help us soar on Summer's wing.

Activities for the Spring Months

PRACTICE your *craft/art/skill* with
dedication, drawing on the inspiration
of your heart.

✳

CLARIFY your life by *spring-cleaning*
surroundings and lifestyle. Check and
reassess your aims and objectives in life.
Bring into focus your plans for the
unfolding year.

✳

REMEMBER all young *life-forms*
and their parents.

✳

IN THIS burgeoning season of life,
meet up with your *spiritual kindred* and
soul-friends whenever possible for mutual
encouragement and fun.

✳

BE AWARE of the *inspirers*, the
door-openers of the spiritual
traditions to which you are drawn.

CREATE a *shrine* to focus your
spiritual intentions.

✳

PLANT *flowers* and *vegetables* for Summer
and Autumn.

✳

WALK and *meditate* outdoors for at least
fifteen minutes daily.

✳

IDENTIFY *five* plants or trees
growing near you.

✳

BE ACTIVE, with like-minded others,
in defending *human rights, world ecology*
or local issues where *injustice*
currently prevails.

✳

AS YOU travel through the land of Spring,
relate your *spiritual journey* to the unfolding
beauty of this season.

MONDAY
m o r n i n g

*I arise today in the name of
the Gatherer of Hope,
the Bringer of Springtime,
the Brightener of Seasons.*

*I kindle my soul at the hearth-fires
of the Kindler of Souls: breath of love,
breath of light,
breath of life,
be upon the embers of my
Spring-wakening soul.
Preserve my soul in gladness
May it flame forth with the sun's
returning glory.*

Bright Mystery, be free as a guest to enter me, always finding a welcome in my heart. All strivings cease when I open the door to you ~ SACRED SILENCE ~ In the secret grove of the heart may we ever meet.

Teacher of my soul, I am inspired every time I contemplate your life. As the world celebrates the coming of Spring, help me to follow the path of my life and walk with me. Give me light to meet the question of this day ~ SOLAR QUESTION.

I remember all newborn creatures about to begin their cycle of life . . . . May they live and love in joyful awareness.

All souls need nurture and the fosterage of encouragement: may the love of the Mother and Father of Soul's Fostering be in my heart, that I may encourage all who are despondent and without hope.

I remember all who have made bad beginnings and now wish to amend their lives, especially . . . . May they receive the blessing of resolution, courage and the willingness to change that the in-dwelling beauty of their lives can shine forth.

*I make the encircling and
go forth today under the
power of the heavens,
light of sun,
radiance of moon,
splendor of fire,
speed of lightning,
swiftness of wind,
depth of sea,
stability of earth,
firmness of rock.
From the heights, to the depths,
may I be encircled in love and safety.*

*May the blessing of the
Gatherer of Hope,
the Bringer of Springtime,
the Brightener of Seasons.
be upon me as I set forth today.
Laughter of the running hours be mine,
and with the leave of lightness, may I come
home in joy.*

50

MONDAY
e v e n i n g

I return home in the name of
the Walker of the Night Stars,
the Guardian of the Hearth,
the Keeper of the Deep Places.

Day darkens, night brightens;
Candle flames, soul lightens;
Day behind me, dreams before:
Open now my soul's door.

Under the tender cloak of night I clarify my soul, out of the searing reach of the wind; without guilt, without shame, without aversion, soul-friends and teachers all, help me clarify this day ~ SELF-CLARIFICATION: I relinquish all the cares and burdens of my day into the deep lap of night. May my soul's teacher reshape them into wider pathways of understanding for me to walk.

Turner of the World, I rejoice in the blessing of your presence. You have been with me during the day even as the stars have been in the sky, obscured by the daylight; although I have not remembered you, you have remembered me. Now, may the peace of your silent blessing enfold me as I enter the companionship of night ~ SACRED SILENCE ~ From the womb of silence, I emerge refreshed and encouraged. May the riches of revelation be seeded in my soul as I turn to contemplate the mysteries of life.

I give thanks to the mighty elements of this planet for their encircling care this day: may their inspiration never fail to kindle our respect as they encircle us.

I give thanks for the gift of life, for I am a unique human being with a soul of great potential: help me to keep its integrity when challenged by the illusions of power.

I ask a blessing on all species of life that are threatened by extinction, especially . . . . May we all respect the precious gift of every life on earth, for each offers an opportunity that may not come again – may peace be upon us all.

May joy, blessing and peace be upon those whom I love, especially upon . . . . .this night.

I smoor* the fire of my soul, as the
Maiden would smoor.
Peace be upon my soul,
peace be to all creatures,
peace be to all upon this planet,
peace be to all that is and was and will be.
Preserve my soul in peace this night,
that it may flame forth brightly
in the still light of dawn.

Walker of the Night Stars,
Guardian of the Hearth,
Keeper of the Deep Places,
May I sleep in you this night.

*Smoor is a Scottish Gaelic term for covering
the fire for the night

51

TUESDAY
morning

Giver of Morning,
Guardian of the Door,
I rise up with you.

I refresh my soul in the showers of Spring,
drop of light, drop of love,
drop of life,
be the blessing on my brow, my heart,
my hands.
May my soul be preserved in peace
from Spring's dawn light,
till Spring's twilight.

Creative Son, Skillful Daughter, between you the shuttle of life brightly runs like a child's colorful game. In the rhythm of your weaving I am enfolded ~ SACRED SILENCE ~ I gratefully put about my shoulders your garment of silence.

Soul-teacher of my love, your helping guidance leads me from ignorance into knowledge, as the chill night is transformed by the glad day; give me assistance to brighten my horizons ~ SOLAR QUESTION.

I am one with all who seek a spiritual pathway through life, especially . . . . May every experience we have today be an opportunity and stepping stone upon our way.

I ask a blessing upon all children who are entering puberty: may the Holy Guardians of each child support and shield their growth at this vulnerable time that each may understand the precious gift of sexual revelation.

The whole world is bringing life to birth at every hour; may all the winter-seeded visions and insights spring freshly into existence this season, especially these ideas and plans that I have fostered . . . .

I do not know what the day will bring: soul-friends all, support me when skies fall, when agreements shatter, when understanding runs out.

I make the encircling of the crafts
about me this Spring day:
delight of poetry,
majesty of music, variety of art,
vision of seership,
compassion of healing,
peace of prayer,
spirit of druidry,
inquiry of science,
transformation of alchemy.
Nine crafts about me,
perfection of skill
encompass my soul this day.

Bestower of Love,
Instructor of Delight,
I am your child this day.

TUESDAY
e v e n i n g

Holy Source,
Ancient Dream,
I return once more to you.

Snow-light turns to Spring-light's
blessing,
bride-lights linger in the sky;
twilight dews the flowers caressing,
vision's gift through soul-veils fly.

As the Spring rises from Winter's fastness, so do I call upon the teacher of my soul to reveal to me the secrets that this day has hidden ~ *SELF-CLARIFICATION* ~ May the revelation of my hidden motivations lead me to better discrimination.

Mirror of Truth, in you all things are revealed and justly answered; although you are just, be also merciful as I enter your clear reflection ~ *SACRED SILENCE* ~ I am dazzled by your beautiful and unchanging stillness; may the light of your truth lead me to the heart of this night's mystery ~ *LUNAR MEDITATION*.

I give thanks for the gift of my abilities, especially for . . . . May I fully respect my gifts and walk their pathways with the help of all the Holy Ones. I thank the encircling powers of the crafts for protecting my soul this day.

I remember all inspirers, artists, musicians, dancers, writers, thinkers and dreamers who gladden the spirit, especially . . . . May they ever keep open the doors between the mundane world and the realms of joy.

There are many who are without mother, father or friend to nurture and encourage them: may the Holy Ones surround them with love and blessing this night.

With the help of the Honer of Vocations, I reconsecrate my being to the discovery and implementation of my life's purpose . . . . May my life be an inspiration to all beings.

I cleanse my soul in the showers of Spring,
light upon my brow,
love upon my heart,
life upon my hands.
May the blessing-drops of Spring
bring peace to the soul of all beings
from Spring's twilight
till Spring's dawn light.

O Dazzling Darkness, be my covering,
O Sparkle of Stars, be my dreaming,
As I wait for Spring's embrace.

Womb of Darkness,
Glimmer of the Dawn,
I arise from your embrace.

◉

I kindle my soul at the
dawn-flowers of Spring,
bud of life,
bud of light,
bud of love,
petals of my heart,
preserve my soul in peace this day,
from day's work to night's play.

Speaker in Silences, spin my heart into your silence as I come before you ~ SACRED SILENCE ~ May I be one with the life of the universe in every breath I take.

As the day brightens and morning sings its lovely song, I turn to you, teacher of my soul; reveal to me the answer of this day's melody ~ SOLAR QUESTION.

I remember all innocent victims of abuse, neglect and violence, especially . . . . May a father's protection rescue them from danger, may a mother's love heal them of their hurts, may the support of friends restore their confidence to live with joy.

Many face insuperable difficulties around the world, especially . . . . Comforter of all Creatures, grant them forthright and courageous hearts in the face of vicissitude.

May I be prepared to set aside or change the plans of this day to follow the urgings of my spiritual service. May I be ever ready to dance with the Spinner of the Universe and to enter into the blessed Land of Youth.

For the needs of all that I love, especially . . . . I ask the help of the Holy Ones.

〰〰〰

I go forth today under the
powers of the planets,
growth of Moon,
energy of Mars,
beauty of Venus,
speed of Mercury,
majesty of Jupiter,
glory of Sun,
silence of Saturn,
innovation of Uranus,
infinity of Neptune.
Nine bright stars to encircle my soul,
from day-spring to nightfall.

☙

The blessing of the Uncreated One
and her child, the Uncreated Light,
be around and about me
from morning to night.

WEDNESDAY
e v e n i n g

Son of the Twilight,
Daughter of Dreams,
Uncreated Child of the Universe,
my heart plays with you.

Spring song broken, heart's token,
candle-message softly spoken;
leaves unfurling, light before,
open now the soul's door.

As Spring awakens all energies from dormancy, so I call upon my soul's teacher to show to me how this day has led me out of isolation . . . . May the passion of awakening life be granted to all who journey through the realm of Spring.

Through the long hours of this day, I have longed to be with you, *Source of Silence.* Bring me now to the depths of your refreshing love ~ SACRED SILENCE ~ From the potent source of stillness I arise to meditate on the moonlight message of your story ~ LUNAR MEDITATION.

I give thanks for the gift of spiritual awareness, and remember . . . . who has helped me on my path: may the lovely light of inner illumination shine upon all pathways and the seekers who walk them.

I remember all who are intolerant and full of prejudice, especially . . . . May the fear that is triggered by the threat of different ways recede as the waters of love and mutual respect rise higher in the planet's prayers.

May all who legislate and decide my country's laws and affairs be gifted with the forbearance and farsightedness not to mar the future.

I give thanks for the powers of the planets that encircled me this day. May their embracing guidance be understood as a token of the universal dance.

I smoor my soul at the eaves of evening:
flower of life,
flower of light,
flower of love,
blossom in peace in the heart of all beings.
From close of night to light of day.

Child of Truth,
Mother of the Word,
Weave your web of sleep about me.

THURSDAY
m o r n i n g

Mother of the Faithful Promise,
Child of the Innocent Day,
Keep me true to my purpose this day.

I drench my soul in the dews of Spring,
dew of light,
dew of love,
dew of life,
refresh my mind, my heart, my being.
May my soul be peacefully preserved
from day's dear light,
till fall of night.

At the rising of the sun, I take refuge in the presence of the Awakener of Spring: as plants bud and creatures prepare for the birth of their young, so do I wait the blossoming of my heart in your stillness ~ SACRED SILENCE ~ May I walk with you this Spring day.

Teacher of my soul and soul-friends all, be to me a beacon of devotion this day as the sun circles its blessing over the wakening world; may my quest be blessed by answers that I can understand with your help ~ SOLAR QUESTION.

I am one with the keepers of integrity, all who guard truth and justice, especially . . . . May judges, arbitrators, leaders and all people remain vigilant in their guardianship of the truth.

I ask a blessing on all children who, through abuse and neglect, have forgotten how to play: may the Holy Innocent Ones of all generations shower upon them the dew of recreation and renewal that their Winter-souls be brought to the glorious resurrection of Spring life.

Be the world so rough, may I never forget the vision of my heart, the dreams of my soul, the creative plans and ideas that quicken my blood and inspire my being, especially . . . .

I make the encircling
of the many-colored winds:
black wind of cold north,
pale green of southwest,
red wind of southeast,
gray wind of northwest,
purple wind of sharp east,
clear wind of the dear west,
speckled wind of northeast,
white wind of warm south,
yellow of the veering wind.
The encompassment of the winds
protect and surround me
this Spring day.

May the blessing of the
Stream of Inspiration,
Fountain of Insight,
attend me as on my way I go.

THURSDAY
e v e n i n g

Health of the Soul,
Keeper of the Heart,
I return this night with you.

Free-born flame in Spring arising,
flickering in the growing dark;
light my spirit's self-disguising,
wake the core of soul's sweet spark.

As the unfolding patterns of Spring strengthen themselves, so I turn to my soul's teacher. Give me grace to see which of my own habitual patterns need to change from the circuit of this one day ~ SELF-CLARIFICATION ~ May I enter a wider arena with the confidence of your help.

Stream of Knowledge, you have filled me with many experiences this Spring day till I am overflowing; now I enter the pool of your quiet patience ~ SACRED SILENCE ~ Refreshing my being in the living waters of universal love, I turn to consider the loving light that illumines the mystery of the night ~ LUNAR MEDITATION.

I give thanks for the gift of health; may that wholeness preserve my life. [OR ... for the gift of sickness, which teaches me respect for my body's wisdom.] May the Healer of Hurts and Fosterer of Health be free to enter my being that it may be in true harmony.

I remember all who are facing death, especially . . . . May they be strengthened by family and soul-friends to prepare for their passing, and may they voyage without fear to their spiritual home assisted by the Holy Ones.

The winds have circled me with their blessing this day: I give thanks for the breath of life that inspirits my being and unites me with the winds that blow.

Fosterer of Innocence, you preserve the integrity of childhood and the integrity of the soul: when faced with the predator who would manipulate truth and violate the soul's innocence, may I look into the mirror of my soul and draw upon the gift of my motherwit to reflect your searching and protective light.

I cleanse my soul in the dews of Spring,
light of mind's refreshing dew,
love of heart's renewing dew,
life of being's restoring dew,
cleanse and recreate my soul this night.
May the souls of all beings be
peacefully preserved
from fall of night
till day's dear light.

Cave of the Heart,
Sanctuary of the Soul,
I sink down into the sleep of repose.

57

❋

Sanctuary of the Soul,
Cave of the Heart,
I come forth from you this Spring day.

◎

I brighten my soul at the threshold
of welcome,
greeting of love,
greeting of life, greeting of light,
inspire my heart, my mind, my body
this Spring day.
May my soul be peacefully preserved
from crown of light to veil of night.

In the holy hollow of my heart
I greet you, Miracle of Mornings.
You have wrought the song of Spring and
bid me sing with you in the silence of
morning ~ SACRED SILENCE ~ May your
song weave my path this day.

Soul-friends and teacher of my
path, show me the way in the darkness when I cannot hear the Spirit's voice;
give me the gift of trust and perseverance
to continue on my way, even as the sun
turns its faithful track ~ SOLAR QUESTION.

I remember those who lack inspiration, who have nothing to look
forward to, especially . . . . May the wells
of blessing be unblocked within their hearts
that the rich gift of life may be restored to
them by the grace of the Holy Ones.

With every beat of my heart, I
acknowledge the gift of compassion that I
have been shown in my life; I remember
and give thanks for . . . . who have
extended unconditional and forgiving love
to me.

As this Spring day unfolds its freedom,
I ask a blessing upon all men who are
imprisoned, without liberty or bound by
onerous obligation or oppressive livelihoods or unemployment that restrict
their souls; may the Holy Living Ones lead
them to heart's freedom and to soul's peace,
and may the soul of manhood be restored
once more.

〰〰〰

I make the encircling of
constellations of Spring:
justice of Virgo,
nurture of Crater,
scrutiny of Boötes,
nobility of Corona Borealis,
courage of Leo,
vigilance of Hydra,
faith of Coma Berenices,
skill of Cancer, questing of Corvus.
Nine constellations
to surround and circle me,
this day without fear.

☘

May the blessing of the
Revealer of Mysteries,
Secret of Sunrise,
be with me this Spring day.

FRIDAY
e v e n i n g

Enfolder of the Night,
Revelation of Evening,
I return in your loving embrace.

Lovely flame, to your source turning,
brightening the dim twilight;
from the stars, forever burning,
bring my heart to birth this night.

As the Spring teaches us to walk the way of burgeoning life, so I call upon my soul's teacher to reveal the pathways of life that I have been walking and growing by this day ~ SELF-CLARIFICATION ~ May I learn to walk the ways of life with confidence and serenity.

As a pilgrim on the path, I turn to you, Keeper of Quests. In the peace of your silence I listen to you ~ SACRED SILENCE ~ Listening to the pulse of the earth, I rejoice in the precious gift of life and ask your help to understand the mystery of this night ~ LUNAR MEDITATION.

I give thanks for my family, for they teach me how to live with truth, especially for . . . . Like the planets of the Milky Way, their influence causes me to constellate my emotions in many different ways – may I remember that I am not the center of the universe, only one star in the whirling galaxy.

I remember all my ancestors, especially . . . . O, all you who have gone before, I receive from you the heritage of life: may all past hindrances be unblocked, may all past fears be assuaged, may all beneficial intentions be fulfilled.

This night I ask a blessing upon all women who are abused, restricted, prey to anxiety and violence, and all for whom this night brings only pain not rest: may the Holy Living Ones shower the blessing of freedom and protection upon them, that the soul of womanhood may be restored once more.

I give thanks for the encircling constellations of the Spring sky: may the Spinner of Galaxies preserve their beauty and may all beings be blessed by their lovely light.

I refresh my soul at the threshold of welcome,
loving rest,
life-giving nurture,
light-bestowing unity,
be upon my heart, my mind,
my body this night.
May the soul of all beings be peacefully
preserved
from veil of night
to crown of light.

The blessing of the Cloak of Night,
the welcome of the Enfolder of Stars,
wrap me around this loving night.

59

SATURDAY
m o r n i n g

Cradle of Morning,
Lap of Mercy,
I rise from your loving embrace
this Spring day.

I anoint my soul with the elixir of healing:
health of truth,
health of nature,
health of knowledge,
be upon my lips, my being, my mind
May health-giving peace be about me,
delivering my soul from danger,
from Spring's true light,
till merciful night.

For the gift of this new morning, I give thanks, Awakener of the Dawn. In dreamful sleep I also am renewed and ready to enter into your loving embrace ~ SACRED SILENCE ~ Keep me true to your sweet song.

Soul-friends and soul's teacher, I call upon you this Spring day; the birds are gathering their nests and tending their young – may I also seek your care as I prepare to deal with the questions of this day ~ SOLAR QUESTION.

I praise the circuit of births by which my life has passed into this existence: ancestors all, companions and kindred many, may your souls be free as the seabirds on the wing, may I ever give thanks for the wisdom of every cell of my body.

For all who are lonely and without friends, especially . . . . I ask a blessing: may the Holy Ones grant the companionship of a soul-friend to all who are without friendship.

This day many rescuers will go into danger to save the lives of people and animals in danger from many other hazards; may the Holy Ones preserve their lives in safe-keeping that rescue be blessedly achieved.

I make the encircling of the
nine great elements:
brightness of sun,
whiteness of moon,
splendor of stars,
swiftness of wind,
warmth of fire,
majesty of thunder,
speed of lightning
profundity of earth,
generosity of sea.
The nine elements
preserve my soul,
surrounding it in peace this Spring day.

May the blessing of the
Prince of the Elements,
the Princess of the Planet,
Surround me
this glad day.

SATURDAY
e v e n i n g

With the blessing of the Star-Kindler,
and the Well-Keeper,
I return home in peace.

Candle flames, day dies,
star-sparkle in the skies;
night's promise gladly bringing
heart's blessing, soul's singing.

As the lengthening light of Spring brightens the world, so I call upon my soul's teacher to ask for light to see what latent power is held within the pool of this day's catch ~ SELF-CLARIFICATION ~ May the salmon of wisdom one day leap within my heart.

Wise Child, Maker of Mysteries, I still the busy chatter of my mind and enter into your peace ~ SACRED SILENCE ~ Your touch awakes the wisdom of my heart's deep well, may I never forget this moment. As the Spring night deepens, so I ask your help to reveal the mystery that I consider this night ~ LUNAR MEDITATION.

As I wonder at the beauty of the world, I offer thanks and blessing from my heart's depths. I give thanks for the places that give me inspiration and continuity of spirit, especially for . . . . I give thanks for the protective encircling of the elements.

I remember all who have no home, all refugees and wanderers, especially . . . . May the Holy Ones lead you to rest and shelter, and the blessing of a happy home.

This night many mourn the loss of loved ones in accidents, many grieve because their dear one's body has not been recovered, many do not even know if the lost one lives still: may the Gatherer of Souls relieve their heart's anxiety and give them sure knowledge and perfect understanding of all that has passed.

As I enter the fastness of night, may the loving protection of the Holy Ones be upon my sleeping; may they conduct me into dreams of wonder and delight; may they greet my soul on waking that I may rise refreshed.

I seal my soul with the elixir of healing:
seal of truth upon my lips,
seal of nature upon my being,
seal of knowledge upon my mind:
the triple blessing of health upon me.
May healing peace be upon the souls of all
beings,
from merciful night
till Spring's true light.

May the blessing of the
Friend of Souls,
the Companion of Hearts,
accompany me this Spring night.

61

SUNDAY
m o r n i n g

Keeper, Maker and Preserver of the Earth,
I rise up remade in you.

I kindle my soul
at the light of the sun:
ray of truth,
ray of knowledge,
ray of nature,
be upon my lips, my mind, my being.
May the triple candle of grace
illuminate and preserve my soul
from lies, from ignorance, from neglect,
this Spring day.

Mirror of Justice, in you is no stain or deception. I ask for the gift of your renewal that I may spring clean my soul in the reflection of your truth ~ SACRED SILENCE ~ May I mediate the divine glory throughout this day.

Teacher of my soul, soul-friends all, with whom I celebrate the unity of life with the green life of the planet as the sun returns from Winter slumber: may the green light transmute each dormant branch, each sleeping seed into the golden sap of life ~ SOLAR QUESTION.

May all who are addicted to deceiving others, may all who suffer from deception, be illuminated by the Mirror of Truth and Justice: may the Holy Ones bring all things into harmony that the clear light of truth shine before the world.

Bright Deliverer, I ask for better trust and confidence in my life, particularly in the area of . . . . May your blessed gift of trust bring me freedom from fear and petty anxiety.

I ask a blessing upon all students and teachers: may the Holy Wise Ones bestow the grace of a receptive mind, the gift of an imaginative soul and the resourcefulness to implement all that is taught and learned.

I encircle myself with the
nine powers of the gifting ones:
ecstasy of energy,
pattern of destiny,
protection of learning,
inspiration of initiation,
challenge of adversary,
liberation of love,
transformation of weaving,
stability of guardianship,
empowerment of wisdom.
Nine encircling breaths
of nine gifting maidens
be my protection this Spring day.

Vision of the Earth
Keeper, Maker and Preserver of the Earth
surround my soul with bliss this day.

SUNDAY
e v e n i n g

Hostel of Welcome,
Hall of Devotion,
under your eaves I come this night.

Dreams grow holy put in action,
work grows fair through starry dreaming,
but where each flows on unmingling,
both are fruitless and in vain.
May the stars within this gleaming,
cause my dreams to be unchained.

The whole Springtime world is shining with raindrops as I call upon my soul's teacher to show to me the living waters that this week have accumulated ~ SELF-CLARIFICATION ~ May insight and imagination triumph in my life.

As I enter the Womb of Darkness, may my soul grow in compassion ~ SACRED SILENCE ~ Forgive my many wanderings from the way you have taught me. You are my guide and way-shower through life and beyond: lead me through this night's mystery ~ LUNAR MEDITATION.

I give thanks for the freedom to tend my gifts, especially my gift of . . . . For the encircling protection of the Holy Keepers of the Cauldron of life's gifts I give great thanks.

I remember all who suffer from addiction, especially . . . . May the

Holy Ones fill the emptiness with joy, love and support that the chains of addiction may be broken.

May this day of recreation bring me closer to the Universal Spirit that sings the song of renewal in all places, in every heart; may there be unity of soul among all beings.

Bright are the blessings that ripen in the fields of dream: may I have true sight and answer to the issues that perplex or move me this night, especially . . . .

I smoor my soul at the twilight of the sun:
gift of truth upon my lips,
gift of knowledge upon my mind,
gift of nature upon my being.
May the triple candle of grace
illuminate and preserve my soul,
and the souls of all beings,
from lies, from ignorance, from neglect,
this Spring night.

Womb of Night,
Cradle of Stars,
I sleep this night in you.

Solar Questions for Imbolc

These questions are part of the morning devotion, to be asked and answered during that time, or to be considered during the day. Some of the answers may reveal aspects of yourself you had not considered, some may require practical implementation. Each day corresponds to the calendrical date, for example: on 15 February, you consult the question on Day 15 below.

~ 1 ~
What is being initiated in your life at this time?

~ 2 ~
How do you practice ecological awareness?

~ 3 ~
What knowledge are you seeking?

~ 4 ~
What news do you wait to hear? What changes will it bring?

~ 5 ~
Is your envy of others obstructing your own achievement?

~ 6 ~
What messages are others trying to tell you?

~ 7 ~
Where is love manifest in your life?

~ 8 ~
What boundaries do you need to pass through?

~ 9 ~
What have you been struggling with and how does it challenge you?

~ 10 ~
How is beauty seeking to express itself in your life?

~ 11 ~
Is complacency clogging up your life?

~ 12 ~
What do you most need and what help is at hand?

~ 13 ~
What significant patterns are emerging from the last year of your life?

~ 14 ~
What enslaves you and how can you be free?

~ 15 ~
Who are you trying to control?

~ 16 ~
What experience of life do you most crave?

~ 17 ~
What message is your body trying to tell you?

~ 18 ~
What do you need to let go of and how is it impeding you?

~ 19 ~
What new concepts are coming into your understanding?
How do they affect your present understanding?

~ 20 ~
Is your criticism undermining someone or something?

~ 21 ~
What needs clarification and what motivations underlie it?

~ 22 ~
In what areas do you need to rest and recover?

~ 23 ~
What memories do you most appreciate?

~ 24 ~
What mutual burdens can you lift from other's backs?

~ 25 ~
What are your dreams telling you?

~ 26 ~
How does your present way of life need to change?

~ 27 ~
What new influences are trying to come into your life?

~ 28 ~
Where is the Spring in your life?

~ 29 ~
Which of your abilities are you neglecting?

~ 30 ~
Are you allowing spontaneity into your life?

~ 31 ~
What needs to be restored and appreciated?

Lunar Meditations for Imbolc

The following meditation subjects may be selected for the appropriate phase of the moon each evening. See the perpetual lunar calendar on p.116.

~ 1 ~
A plant or flower of your choice.

~ 2 ~
The things that inspire you.

~ 3 ~
Memory of childhood games.

~ 4 ~
The gifts of Spring.

~ 5 ~
Your kinship with humanity.

~ 6 ~
Meditate upon truth.

~ 7 ~
A story of your choice that moves you.

~ 8 ~
The welcome of like-souled friends.

~ 9 ~
The blessing of fire.

~ 10 ~
The vista through the window of imagination.

~ 11 ~
The itinerary of your spiritual quest.

~ 12 ~
The compassion of memory.

~ 13 ~
The invitation sent by your dreams.

~ 14 ~
The inheritance of your blood.

~ 1 5~
The integrity of your vocation.

~ 16 ~
The gift of grace.

~ 17~
The release of forgiveness.

~ 18~
The promise of horizons.

~ 19 ~
Your relationship to your country.

~ 20 ~
The blessing of rain.

~ 21 ~
Meditate upon a poem that enlivens your spirit.

~ 22 ~
The service of parenthood.

~ 23 ~
Your spiritual quest thus far.

~ 24 ~
The perseverance and power of heart's desire.

~ 25 ~
The gift of love.

~ 26 ~
The song of Spring's new life.

~ 27 ~
The silent testimony of innocence in the face of tyranny.

~ 28 ~
A tree of your choice.

~ 29 ~
The compassionate surrender of night.

BELTANE

THE SUMMER *quarter of Beltane brings the gift of increased confidence and is a time of growth and greater sociability as the weather grows fine and hot. It is traditionally the time for celebrating the essential eros of the year, the vitality of Summer and the joys of youth. In the human growth cycle it corresponds to the period of young adulthood when the blood is hot, when ideas are sometimes impetuous and ambitions pursued with vigor and ardor. Beltane is a good time to celebrate the lives of all heroes and heroines, all protectors of the land, all who were involved in innovative and resourceful means of help, all holy ones whose great love complements their spiritual practice with human grace.*

FOR THE WEEKS BETWEEN
1 MAY AND 31 JULY

Greetings and Farewells during Beltane

SONG OF BELTANE

I am the calm, I am the quickening,
I am the intoxication and the force,
I am the silence, I am the singer,
I am the stallion galloping to its source.
I am the bright pavilion and the feasting,
I am the wedding couple and the bed,
I am the morning chorus and the heartbeat,
I am the goal to which all paths are led.

THRESHOLD INVOCATION
FOR THE FESTIVAL OF BELTANE

(to be said at the front door of the house on the
eve of Beltane, 30 April, in the evening)

Maiden of Flowers, open the door,
Smith of souls, come you in.
Let there be welcome to the growing strength,
Let there be welcome to the Summer of the Year.
In bud and blossom you are traveling,
In fruit and fragrance you will arrive.
May the blessed time of Beltane
Inflame the soul of all beings,
Bringing energy and effort to conflagration.
From the depths to the heights,
From the heights to the depths,
In the core of every soul.

GREETING TO THE SUMMER SOLSTICE (21 June)

Glory of the Day-Star, hail!
    Lifter of the Light, Burnisher of the Sky.
Gifts of love to earth are bringing,
    Summer's shimmer, dew's delight.
Dancing be the heart within us,
    Open be our souls to bliss,
Courage vanquish every shadow,
    Greet midsummer with a kiss.

FAREWELL TO THE SEASON OF BELTANE

(to be said at the back door/window of the house on
the last morning of Beltane, 31 July)

Go with thanks and go with blessing,
    Season of vitality.
Souls with life are deeply freighted
    Hearts are full of energy.
Under bud and blossom traveling,
    You have come to Summer's growth.
Soul-Smith, who has forged this brightness,
    Flower-Maid, whose lips have kissed,
Touch the hidden fruit within us,
    Bring us into Autumn's bliss.

Activities for the Summer Months

PRACTICE your *physical skills*
e.g. sport/exercise/dance, etc. drawing upon
the vigor of this season.

❋

REGULARLY assess your *motivations* and
your use of the gift of life.

❋

REMEMBER *spiritual kindred* – those
whose spiritual focus you share.

❋

IN THIS busy season, make time for
proper *soul-nurture*.

❋

BE AWARE of the *heroes* and *heroines*
who have made the spiritual pathways
come alive for you.

❋

PLANT and plan your garden to
provide a *treasury of color* in late
Summer and Autumn.

WALK and *meditate* outdoors for
at least half an hour daily.

✳

IDENTIFY *flowers* and *animals* in
your locality and learn about their life
and habitat.

✳

CREATE a *spontaneous dance* that
physically expresses your kinship with
the universe.

✳

BE ACTIVE with like-minded others, in
providing *support* for *environmental concerns*
both at local and global levels.

✳

AS YOU travel through the country of
Summer, relate your *spiritual journey* to the
bright gifts of this season.

MONDAY
m o r n i n g

PRACTICE FOR EACH MONDAY IN BELTANE

From the Breast of Beauty,
out of the Lap of Peace,
I rise up refreshed.

I kindle my soul at the forge
of the Soul-Smith,
spark of life,
spark of love,
spark of light,
companion my quest this day
till I come home at twilight.

Companion of my Soul, Friend of my Heart, in the secret place of my heart, I come to you ~ SACRED SILENCE ~ May I never forget the closeness of your presence.

As the melody of summer drenches the land in its sweetness, I call upon my soul-teacher to help me find the descant to the question of this day ~ SOLAR QUESTION.

As I start my week of work, I dedicate the work of my hands for the following intention . . . . May the craft and mastery of my daily work enhance the great weaving of the universe.

Liberator of Souls, assist and release all who are imprisoned in spirals of violent abuse: both those who perpetrate abuse and those who receive it. May the shackles of anger and resentment be transformed into the loving bonds of peace and understanding.

May the beauty of each soul blossom as the Spirit awakens all life this Summer morning.

I weave the cincture of protection
From the nine powers of nine flowers:
beauty of rose,
triumph of daffodil,
loyalty of honeysuckle,
simplicity of primrose,
majesty of iris,
humility of violet,
radiance of crocus,
luminance of lily,
innocence of daisy:
nine powers of nine flowers
about me this day.

Companion of my Soul,
Friend of my Heart,
I go forth with you.

MONDAY
e v e n i n g

Companion of my Soul,
Friend of my Heart,
I come home to you.

Nightfall, heart's call, summer light lifting;
rainfall, bird call, white blossom drifting;
candlelight kindles soul-bright gifting.

I seize the light of illumination and ask my soul's teacher for courage to review the day without blame: ~ *SELF-CLARIFICATION* ~ may all that is tangled be made straight.

Teller of Tales, while this summer day has been unfolding, I have been keeping your story safe within me. Now, in the silence of my heart, I share it once again with you ~ *SACRED SILENCE* ~ May my story run true to its homing. As night beckons, help me to follow the mystery that shines in the darkness ~ *LUNAR MEDITATION*.

The mind has as many turnings as a maze: may all who have been confused within its labyrinthine windings, may all who suffer from mental illness, receive healing, restoration and gentle mindfulness through the mercy of the Lifter of Veils.

I give thanks for the revelation of daily life: the small and wondrous events that have tracked this day, especially . . . .

In the darkness of doubt, may I ever remember the three candles that illumine every darkness: the candles of truth, nature and knowledge.

I give thanks to the protection of flowers: may the Summer-ripening fruits draw strength and enduring seed-life from your scent and beauty.

As I prepare to sleep, I bring these intentions to the Holy Ones . . . . May the needs of all who seek help and strength be brought by you into the care of the Granter of Dreams.

I smoor my soul with the care of
the Soul-Smith,
shape of life,
shape of love,
shape of light,
be upon all beings in quest for peace,
both now and then and in times to come.

Gatherer of the Night,
Shaper of Stars,
I sink to rest in you.

✷

TUESDAY
m o r n i n g

PRACTICE FOR EACH TUESDAY IN BELTANE

Opener of Morning,
Source of Recreation,
I rise up refreshed this morning.

☺

I kindle my soul from the light of
Summer's glory:
truth in my heart,
strength in my hands,
singleness of purpose in my mind;
the triune powers of
light, life and love
be my soul's companions
this Summer day.

Faithful to my word, I open my heart
to you anew, Keeper of the Heart
~ SACRED SILENCE ~ Mighty Mystery, I
am recreated through the touch of your
peace.

Teacher of my soul, you sang the
faithful song of your life with joy
and courage, give me clarity of mind as
I now consider the transforming question
of this day ~ SOLAR QUESTION.

From the depths of holy silence,
I give thanks for the joy and energy
of life. May all beings enjoy the
vitality of their existence.

I remember all who suffer great pain
and long-term illness, especially . . . .
May the Healer of Hurts breathe balm and

restoration into all wounded lives.

May all negative, angry and harmful
attitudes, especially my . . . . that I
harbor within me be transformed into new
and available life.

The dance of a Summer day calls my
steps: may I respond to the rhythm and
melody of its music.

〰〰〰

I weave the cincture of protection
from the nine threads of life:
peace of mind,
truth of speech
timeliness of action,
success of deed,
prosperity of work,
health of body,
courage of spirit,
compassion of heart,
wisdom of soul.
These nine threads be my belt
Wherever I walk.

☘

May the blessing of
the Strong Protector,
the Bringer of Summer,
the Spinner of the the the Day-Star,
be upon me as I set forth today.
Beauty of the glad day be mine,
And with the beatitude of brightness,
May I come home in joy.

TUESDAY
e v e n i n g

I return in the name of
the Maker, Keeper and Lover of all life.
I return in the presence of
the Holy Ones,
protectors of my soul.

Candle burning, light unbending,
soul turning, heart befriending,
spirit's beacon never-ending.

I give thanks for the alchemy of
change by which all life's experiences transmute my fixed viewpoints into
new perceptions of possibility. With the
help of my soul's teacher, I review this day
and the changes it has brought ~ SELF-
CLARIFICATION ~ May all these changes
bring my soul into truer alignment with
the Divine Spirit.

Maker, Keeper and Lover of all life,
I turn to you: I am marvelously
made, protectingly kept, gloriously loved
by you throughout this day. I pass from
speech into silence now, that you may
speak in the wonder of my heart ~ SACRED
SILENCE.

From the depths of Vessel of
Recreation, I am forged anew, Smith
of Souls. Give me light to consider
the mystery of this lunar phase ~ LUNAR
MEDITATION.

In the busy tracks of the world, I
remember all whose energy is
burned out or extinguished by overwork:
may they receive the gifts of rest and recreation so that they may once more be able
to respect the powers and limitations of
their being.

I give thanks for the nine interweaving
threads of life that have surrounded me
this day: may my whole being be infused
with the strength and sureness of the
growing year.

May political prisoners and those
imprisoned because of their courageous
championing of the innocent and disempowered be strengthened and enheartened
by the presence of the Holy Ones.

I smoor my soul as the light fades,
peace in my heart,
peace upon my hands,
peace in my mind.
May the triune powers of
light, life and love
bless and preserve all beings
this night and every night.

Maiden of Sky-Flowers,
Faithful Companion of the Night,
under the running laughter of the clouds,
under the shining mirror of the moon
I lie down in peace with you.

WEDNESDAY
morning

Lady of Laughter,
Lord of the Shining Brow,
I rise up with you.

I lave my soul in the everlasting waters:
drop of light,
drop of life,
drop of love,
be upon my brow, be upon my tongue,
be upon my heart.
May my soul be preserved
from crack of light
till fall of night.

Turner of the Seasons' Wheel, while I have slept you have been hastening Summer. Before I enter into the motion of the day-star, I rest in the stillness of the wheel's turning ~ *SACRED SILENCE.*

O . . . . , teacher of my soul, kindle in me the enthusiasm that makes life's path a joyous thing; may I not stint any being of this share in the abundance of life, but ever encourage and support all I meet today to reach their full potential. Give me help to answer the questions of this day ~ *SOLAR QUESTION.*

May I have the daring and audacity to travel my spiritual path to its very heart: to keep open the approaches, that the Beauty of the Universe may shine forth.

Reconciler of Hearts, create concord between men and women that we may learn to weave with equal delight the shuttle of male and female upon the looms of life.

May all eyes be open to the transforming delight of Summer this day; may the earth be made glad by the dance of life, may we discern the blessed peace of the Plain of Delight upon our planet.

I weave the cincture of protection
from the powers of the senses:
vision of sight,
sureness of smell,
resonance of hearing,
discrimination of taste,
sensitivity of touch,
clarity of speech,
beauty of understanding,
sharpness of instinct,
empathy of heart.
Nine powers about me
to gird and protect me,
on the pathways that I walk.

May the blessing of the Bright One,
the Brightener of Mornings,
be upon me and on all I love.
Laughter of the running hours be mine,
and with the brow of brightness may I come
home in joy.

WEDNESDAY
e v e n i n g

Gatherer of Dew,
Summoner of Night,
under the eaves of evening,
under the flight of swallows,
I come home to you.

Weft-light, warp-light, looms of evening,
moth-flight, heart's sight, sleep's conceiving,
shuttle hastening soul's retrieving.

The universe teems with a myriad of ideas and thoughts that have been lost in this day's business. Teacher of my soul, please give me grace to gather my scattered thoughts and understand my motivations and desires ~ SELF-CLARIFICATION ~ May I be mindful of the creative possibilities that every day offers.

O Uncreated Beauty, I turn once more to your embrace. In homage, I offer . . . . (a deed, thought, realization of this day) to you, Beloved of my heart. Now in silence, I open my arms and listen to your words of loving wisdom ~ SACRED SILENCE ~ In your sweet embrace I am lovingly restored. Beloved Beauty who binds the universe in one free bond of love, give me light to lovingly comprehend the mystery of this night ~ LUNAR MEDITATION.

In the veils between the worlds, I remember the faery folk who guard the ancient places; may we walk lightly and with courtesy upon the earth, may no being stay their progress or block their path, that the hidden household of the earth may be peaceful.

When life's weaving becomes tangled, may the Untangler of Threads help all threads run smoothly in the tapestry of life.

I give thanks for the powers of the senses that have protected my path this day.

The Summer sun can shine so strong that we are driven into the shade: may those who have too much zeal, who want to convert everyone to their own way, learn to temper their fierce beliefs so that seekers are not driven from their path.

I bathe my soul in the everlasting waters:
mercy of light upon my brow,
mercy of life upon my tongue,
mercy of love upon my heart.
The Mercy of Mercies upon every being,
from fall of night,
till crack of light,
in the perfection of peace.

Cloak of Stars,
Mantle of the Night,
Hastener of Dreams,
may I be safe enfolded this summer night.

79

THURSDAY
m o r n i n g

Revealer of Dreams,
Opener of Morning,
I rise up with you this morning.

◉

I freshen my soul in the airs of Summer,
breeze of life,
breeze of love,
breeze of light,
awaken my breath, my heart, my vision.
May my soul be peacefully preserved
from Summer day to Summer night.

Sacred Source of Life, you orchestrate the elements in one great symphony of life, the wild and untamed tempests and the quiet showers alike; within the silence of my soul, I come into the still center of your peace ~ SACRED SILENCE.

Teacher of my soul, dear . . . . , may the blessing of life be the breath of believing as I trustfully turn to you. Help me to trust the answers that arise as I consider the question of this day ~ SOLAR QUESTION.

For the unwanted, the disfigured, the wounded ones who go unnoticed in all places of the world, I call upon the Companion of Comfort and the Holy Ones to ease their isolation and their pain.

Promises are given life by those who act them: may I be ever loyal to the deep commitments of my life, especially to . . . .

May those who are sitting examinations at this time be assisted by the Holy Ones to success.

May there be peace and concord among all nations in conflict, especially in . . . . May all who are embattled achieve the victory of understanding their opponents with compassion.

I weave the cincture of protection
from the paths of the pilgrim:
aspiration of heights,
guidance of star-paths,
dryness of deserts,
clarity of clearings,
refreshment of wells,
choice of crossroads,
shade of forest-paths,
wisdom of caves,
deepness of depths.
Nine pathways to guide and protect me
on the ways I shall walk this day.

May the blessing of the Flower Bride,
and the Groom of Gladness attend me.
Married to the morning,
wed to the sun's circuit,
I take my course this day.

THURSDAY
e v e n i n g

Singer of Summer,
Musician of the Meadowlands,
I sing my song to you.

Well of gladness, deeply springing,
notes of mercy and of life,
shimmer forth on candle's bringing,
healing soul of body's strife.

May I have the humility of the bare earth, which doesn't pretend to be anything other than itself, as I look back at how I have revealed my soul today ~ SELF-CLARIFICATION ~ Teacher of my soul, remind me when I become self-important to realize that I am but a part of the vast tapestry of life and not its main design.

Beloved Guardian of Life, I am gathered once more to the place of peace, to the shrine of my heart ~ SACRED SILENCE ~ After the scattering of this Summer day, you gather my life in a sacred way; help now to understand the mystery that you have created ~ LUNAR MEDITATION.

The world's abundance swells as Summer sings its lovely song, though I often sing a song of need. I bring these needs to mind now . . . . May any hint of want or lack be ever greeted by the hospitality of the Great Provider.

I give thanks for the beauty of the earth; may all who pollute and despoil its fair face so experience the wonder and restoration of nature that they may come to better understanding and respect.

For all who are wandering far from home, in exile, confusion or despair, especially . . . . May the Holy Ones accompany their wanderings and lead to them to the hospitality of the human heart and the deep abiding comfort of the Holy Earth.

I give thanks to the pathways of the pilgrim for protecting my pilgrim path this day: may my soul be ever led to the sacred thresholds of spiritual wisdom.

I quieten my soul under the airs of Summer,
peace upon my breath,
peace upon my heart,
peace upon my vision,
the peace of peace upon each being,
this Summer night.

Chorus of Constellations,
Dancer of the Spiral Galaxy,
Diviner of Dreams,
may I dance and sing with you this night.

Kindler of Dawn,
Spirit of Summer,
I rise up with you,
under winds and waters,
under hills and heavens,
this Summer day.

I illuminate my soul with the gift of sunlight:
ray of love, ray of light, ray of life,
be upon my heart, my brow, my limbs.
May my soul be preserved
from morning's break
to twilight's falling.

Hearer of Prayers, you know what moves my heart. Before I set forth to accomplish the deeds of this day, I tune my heart to your music ~ SACRED SILENCE ~ May I learn to trust your constant help.

Faithful companion, teacher of my soul, all souls take the way that they best know; lead me where my soul shall be inspired to seek fresh transformations, as I search for the answer to the issues of today ~ SOLAR QUESTION.

I dedicate my energies to the benefit of the universe this day. When enthusiasm wanes, when life seems dull and savorless, may the Holy Ones send fresh inspiration for the way.

As the birds are raising their nestlings and young animals learn the patterns of life through play, I ask for that same playfulness to enliven my life and bring lightness of heart to those whom I love, especially to. . . . .

All things living have their rest and ending, may all who are woven into patterns of predatory vengeance, of terrorism, vendetta, mafia, or feud, be released from the heritage of hatred.

I weave the cincture of protection
from the powers of the Summer
Constellations:
energy of Sagittarius,
enchantment of Lyra,
clarity of Aquila,
subtlety of Scorpio,
healing of Ophiucus,
equity of Libra,
help of Delphinus,
beauty of Cygnus,
strength of Hercules.
Nine constellations
to gird and protect me,
as I go forth this day.

May the blessing of the Soul-Smith,
the brightness of the Flower Maid,
be upon my path this glad day.

FRIDAY
e v e n i n g

Queen of Quietness,
Sovereign of the Stars,
I come home under the long eaves
of Summer,
on the song of birds
to the abode of peace.

Brightlight, soul-light,
candlelight quickening,
hold fast, soul's-night deep light brightening,
Soul's-flight waits for heart's light gathering.

I have traveled the week in trust and travail. My soul's teacher, help me to clarify and bring order to the muddle of the week ~ *SELF-CLARIFICATION* ~ Into your hands I commit the burdens and unresolved issues of this week: as I sleep, may the Holy Ones give me insight and help to bring them to resolution.

Holy Mystery, I come in quietness to the hearth of rejoicing, where your sacred fire ever burns. I enter the hospitality of your heart ~ *SACRED SILENCE* ~ Warmed at the hearth of joy, I joyfully turn to consider the mystery of this night ~ *LUNAR MEDITATION*.

May all who are journeying this night find their true haven and their soul's rest: may the Winged Messengers guide their steps in the darkness.

When things go wrong and seem unmendable, when despair threatens, may I go forward trusting in the guidance of my soul-friends, especially . . . .

I give thanks for the protection of the Summer constellations this day: may their glorious light inspire courage and fearless trust in the Provider of the Universe.

May all who are in anxiety and trouble find the calm encircling love of Comforter of Hearts, especially . . . .

I smoor my soul under the shade of night:
veil of love upon my heart,
veil of light upon my brow,
veil of life upon my limbs.
The veil of rest upon every being,
from fall of night,
till call of light.

Queen of Quietness,
Sovereign of the Stars,
I take my rest in you.

SATURDAY
m o r n i n g

Lifter of the Light,
Emboldener of Hearts,
I rise up with you on wings of courage.

I fire my soul at the forge of the Soul-Smith:
pulse of life,
pulse of light,
pulse of love,
shape the splendor of my
summer-wakening soul.
Preserve my soul in joyful strength,
may it glow with the glory of the
Summer's sun.

Maker of Mornings, I seize the confidence of this Summer morning to
enter into the stillness of silence and greet
you ~ SACRED SILENCE ~ Your presence
warms my heart and guards my way: I
thank you for the gift of life.

O teacher of my soul, as the light
lengthens, so do I call upon your aid
to reveal the meaning of today's question ~
SOLAR QUESTION ~ May the unfolding of
the seasons help me to grow in maturity
and manifest the revelations of my
~ SOLAR QUEST.

I remember all parents of miscarried
or stillborn children: may their loss
be no less mourned, may their love be no
less valued than if their child had grown

up. May the Divine Mother and Father of
all Life, receive the souls of these young
ones and comfort the grieving parents.

May the Holy Guardians encompass
all places of sanctuary and protection, all
places of retreat, healing and restoration of
spirit, that those seeking enclaves of quiet
peace may find healing of soul.

I dedicate the plans, ideas that I
intend to focus upon this day and work,
especially . . . .

I weave the cincture of protection:
protection of animals
around and about me:
might of mane,
power of horn,
singleness of eye,
breadth of fin,
swiftness of wing,
strength of heart,
speed of limb,
sureness of hoof,
beauty of shape.
Creature-companions,
encompass me wherever I go.

The blessing of
the Lifter of the Light,
the Emboldener of Hearts,
be upon me this day as I go forth.
May the light of Spirit be lifted in every place,
that all hearts be emboldened for the good.

SATURDAY
e v e n i n g

Gatherer of Night,
Healer of Hearts,
I come home to you;
In the presence of the Holy Ones,
Companioned by . . . .
(spiritual teacher)

Sunlight falling, moonlight calling,
soul-fire kindled in the dark;
shadows falling, spirits calling,
soul-fire from the hidden spark.

At the close of day, I call upon the teacher of my soul to help clear the way between me and the Eternal Freedom ~ *SELF-CLARIFICATION* ~ May I never try to limit the universe by my own narrow horizons.

Soul-friends all, keepers of my quest, I thank you for your help along the way. As peace descends upon the blessed night, I enter into the silence of the Universal Heart ~ *SACRED SILENCE* ~ I am lovingly restored to the rhythm of the universe. O Gatherer of Night, there is no darkness that you do not illuminate, please show to me the beauty of your moon-bright wisdom as I contemplate ~ *LUNAR MEDITATION.*

I give thanks to the creature-companions who have protected me today:

may your girdle of protection remind me that the same life threads us through with strength and endurance. I remember especially those creatures whose thread of life can now be barely traced in the great tapestry of creation: . . . . May your special gifts be cherished and acknowledged by more generous hearts.

As the earth circles, I celebrate all who strive to help the disempowered, especially . . . . ; may the Opener of Freedom assist their struggle that all beings may enjoy life and liberty.

I rejoice in the greening earth, in the burgeoning of projects and ideas, in the growth of friendships and associations: as Summer fields ripen with the grain of life, so may all that is in my heart come to maturity.

I smoor my soul,
as the Soul-Smith would smoor.
Peace be upon my soul,
peace be to all creatures,
peace be to all upon this planet,
peace be to all that is and was and will be.
Preserve my soul in restful peace this night
that it may be new-forged in morning's glory.

Womb of Night,
Companion of the Stars,
Cradle of Quietness, Star-Quilt of Splendor,
into your embrace I am coming.

85

Lady who brightens the door,
Lord who emboldens the heart,
I rise up with you.

I kindle my soul at the shrine of the sun,
flame of light,
flame of love,
flame of life,
be upon my intentions, my emotions,
my being.
Triple spark of sunlight,
illuminate my soul and preserve it
this bright Summer day.

Keeper of the Cauldron of Life, you have mixed and shaped me as I am. Before I go forth into the recreation of Summer, I acknowledge your presence in every cell of my being ~ SACRED SILENCE.

Teacher of my soul, in your life you asked many questions in order to straighten your path, grant me the essential curiosity to ask such questions, and give me help now to find an answer to today's issue ~ SOLAR QUESTION.

The sacred laws of hospitality bid us welcome the guest as a member of our own family: may all beings of goodwill who will come within the compass of my daily round today experience welcome and the hospitality of my heart.

I remember all who are suffering prejudice because of cultural origin or religious background, especially . . . . : may the blinkers of bigotry be lifted and the vision of the compassionate heart prevail.

May the blessed space of this day open my eyes afresh to all that the world has yet to unfold. May the embrace of festival and rejoicing warm whatever is cold, encourage whatever is weak, enliven whatever is slow to come to life within me.

I weave the cincture of protection,
from the nine powers of nine trees,
strength of oak,
straightness of ash,
purity of birch,
absorbency of alder,
brightness of beech,
elegance of elm,
healing of willow,
power of holly,
everlastingness of yew.
Nine trees to circle me,
nine powers to guard me,
as the Summer song resounds.

May the blessing of the Brightener of Doors,
the Emboldener of Hearts,
lead me over new thresholds this glad day.

SUNDAY
e v e n i n g

Radiance of Summer,
Keeper of the Flame,
I return home on the tides of Summer peace.

Sun's song, moon's song, starlight lifting,
mind's rest, heart's quest, long time drifting,
come to source of soul's deep sifting.

I come before the Everlasting Power of Spirit to ask for help to see in what ways I have served the universe today: in what ways have I taken power to myself or manipulated it; in what ways have I respected the power of Spirit ~ SELF-CLARIFICATION.

Cauldron of Creation, mixer and melder of souls, I return to the stillness of your center ~ SACRED SILENCE ~ May I be enabled to face the challenges arising in the week ahead with your creative help. I pass from the source of silence to the place of contemplation as the moon rises to illumine the night ~ LUNAR MEDITATION.

May the mundane systems, institutes and governments of the world encourage, protect and reward the creative imagination for the better good of the universe.

I give thanks to the powers of the trees for their protection this day: may the trees also be protected and preserved from wanton scathe and senseless harm.

To all the companions of my soul, the Holy Ones, my soul's teacher, the friends, animals, plants, trees and places who have offered me refreshment of spirit: may they be eternally blessed and celebrated.

I gather into one bountiful embrace my dear ones, especially . . . . May the Holy Ones protect and sustain them wherever they go.

I shrine my soul in the shrine of the moon,
beam of light upon my intentions,
beam of love upon my emotions,
beam of life upon my being.
Triple beam of moonlight,
illuminate the soul of all beings,
within the shrine of sleep.

I am sinking onto the Breast of Beauty,
into the Lap of Peace,
I am being carried by the everlasting
arms of desire
into the depths of sleep.

Solar Questions for Beltane

These questions are part of the morning devotion, to be asked and answered during that time, or to be considered during the day. Some of the answers may reveal aspects of yourself you had not considered, some may require practical implementation. Each day corresponds to the calendrical date, for example: on 25 June, you consult the question on Day 25 below.

~ 1 ~
What creative possibilities are surfacing at this time?

~ 2 ~
What fears are holding you back? What weakness do they hide?

~ 3 ~
Where do you need to allow growth in your life?

~ 4 ~
Which of your dreams do you most want to come true?

~ 5~
Where are your energies overextended?

~ 6 ~
What pattern is emerging from your spiritual path to date?

~ 7 ~
What is the source of the vital power within you?

~ 8 ~
What broken or fragmentary parts of your life need mending?

~ 9 ~
*What old story are you telling against yourself? What new story waits
to be told?*

~ 10 ~
Where do you hurt and why? Where does healing lie?

~ 11 ~
Who do you need to forgive most?

~ 12 ~
What do you appreciate most about your life?

~ 13 ~
What ambitions wait to be fulfilled in your life?

~ 14 ~
How are you limiting yourself at present?

~ 15 ~
What is preying on your mind?

~ 16 ~
What makes you most angry? Why?

~ 17 ~
What challenges are on the horizon?

~ 18 ~
What do you need to learn or master at this time?

~ 19 ~
What sacrifices must you make to fulfill your plans?

~ 20 ~
Are you respecting or abusing trust?

~ 21 ~
What is the source of your courage?

~ 22 ~
Which of your senses is most weak? Exercise it today.

~ 23 ~
Where is the warmth in your life?

~ 24 ~
In which areas of your life are you self-important?

~ 25 ~
Are you misusing responsibility or power?

~ 26 ~
Are you properly prepared for emergency action?

~ 27 ~
Are you respecting or abusing rest and recreation time?

~ 28 ~
Where do you need to exercise self-discipline most?

~ 29 ~
Which special gifts and abilities are you neglecting?

~ 30 ~
How can you bring simplicity and shape to your muddle?

~ 31 ~
Which of your neglected friends would most enjoy hearing from you?

Lunar Meditations for Beltane

The following meditation subjects may be selected for the appropriate phase of the moon each evening. See the perpetual lunar calendar on p.116 for the correct phase.

~ 1 ~
The support of friendship

~ 2 ~
The messages of your body.

~ 3 ~
Lovers you have lost and found.

~ 4 ~
Peace and concord among earth's nations.

~ 5 ~
Abundance in your life.

~ 6 ~
Projects you most wish to come to fruition.

~ 7 ~
The complementarity of women and men.

~ 8 ~
The skills that you possess.

~ 9 ~
The wisdom of nature.

~ 10 ~
Growth in your emotional life.

~ 11 ~
The gift of eros.

~ 12 ~
Happiness.

~ 13 ~
The rhythms and cycles of the moon in your life.

~ 14 ~
The secret country of dreams.

~ 15 ~
Your heart's desire.

~ 16 ~
The blessing of the earth.

~ 17 ~
Partnerships in your life.

~ 18 ~
The messages of birdsong.

~ 19 ~
The company of solitude.

~ 20 ~
The thing you must dare to do now.

~ 21 ~
The shores of home.

~ 22 ~
The role of ecstasy in your life.

~ 23 ~
The scent of flowers.

~ 24 ~
The beauty of the enduring stars.

~ 25 ~
The strength and beauty of the little things.

~ 26 ~
The richness of your inner treasury.

~ 27 ~
Your special place of peace and refreshment.

~ 28 ~
The song of night.

~ 29 ~
The times when things seemed hopeless but came right.

LUGHNASADH

T HE AUTUMN *quarter of Lughnasadh brings the gift of maturity and is a time of physical harvest and spiritual garnering. It sees the greatest change in weather from broiling heat to dark and chilly nights. It is the time for celebrating the harvest and sees the busy preparations for winter. In the human growth cycle, Lughnasadh corresponds to the period of mature adulthood when a certain steadiness and responsibility have been established. It is a good time to celebrate the lives of all who have helped stabilize and uphold the noble values of life, of all who have exercised good judgment and steered the doubtful into the harbor of certainty, of all holy ones whose guardianship has saved us from life-disabling mistakes.*

FOR THE WEEKS BETWEEN
1 AUGUST AND 31 OCTOBER

Greetings and Farewells during Lughnasadh

THE SONG OF LUGHNASADH

I am the sovereign splendor of creation,
  I am the fountain in the courts of bliss,
I am the bright surrender of the willpower,
  I am the watchful guardian and the kiss.
I am the many-colored landscape,
  I am the transmigration of the geese,
I am the burnished glory of the breastplate,
  I am the harbor where all strivings cease.

THRESHOLD INVOCATION
FOR THE FESTIVAL OF LUGHNASADH

(to be said at the front door of the house on the
eve of Lughnasadh, 31 July, in the evening)

Lady of the Land, open the door,
Lord of the Forest, come you in.
Let there be welcome to the bountiful compassion,
  Let there be welcome to the Autumn of the Year.
In fruit and grain you are traveling,
  In ferment and bread you will arrive.
May the blessed time of Lughnasadh
  Nourish the soul of all beings,
Bringing love and healing to all hurts.
  From the heights to the depths,
From the depths to the heights,
  To the wounds of every soul.

GREETING TO THE AUTUMN EQUINOX
(21 September)

Hail! Journeyer of the Heavens,
    Queen of Brightness, King of Beauty!
Gifts of gladness richly bringing,
    Autumn sheaves and red leaves' fall.
Generous be the heart within us,
    Open be our hands to all,
Justice to be in equal measure,
    Harvest thankfulness our call.

FAREWELL TO THE SEASON OF LUGHNASADH

(to be said at the back door/window of the house on
the last morning of the Lughnasadh quarter, 31 October)

Go with thanks and go with blessing,
    Season of soul's nurturing.
Souls with fruit are deeply freighted,
    Hearts are healed rejoicingly.
As ripened fruit and grain have traveled
    You have come to Autumn's barn.
Forest Lord, whose clearings echo,
    Sovereign Lady, who has poured,
Touch the hidden mystery in us,
    Aid us to find Winter's hoard.

Activities for the Autumn Months

PRACTICE your *knowledge, learn new subjects, relate new information* to your existing store of wisdom.

❉

ASSESS your own *life's harvest*: prepare fallow areas of your life for reseeding, clear old fields of overgrowth.

❉

REMEMBER your own descendants and carefully prepare your *spiritual heritage* and physical bequest to them.

❉

FOLLOW the *inspirational pathways* that lead you to the heart of your art or skill.

❉

MAKE *peace* or bring the *concord of resolution* between yourself and opponents.

❉

HARVEST *fruit* and *vegetables* and prepare the garden for winter.

B E AWARE of the leaders and guardians
who have protected the *pathways of
compassion* by their sacrifice or action, and
incorporate aspects of their example into
your own lifestyle.

❀

W ALK and *meditate* outdoors for at least
fifteen minutes daily.

❀

I DENTIFY *plants* and *trees* by their
Autumn color and find out about their
habitats and qualities.

❀

B E ACTIVE with like-minded others, in
bringing *healing* or *relief* to living beings in
distress, whether human, animal, plant, etc.

❀

A S YOU travel through the country of
Autumn, relate your *spiritual journey* to the
rich gifts available at this time.

MONDAY
morning

Mother of Mercy,
Father of Faithfulness,
I rise up this day.

I clothe my soul in the
mantle of creation,
heavens of light,
earth of life,
seas of love,
surround and support my
Autumn-wakening soul.
Preserve my soul in compassion,
may it shine forth with the rich Autumn
sunlight.

Lady of Splendor, Lord of Glory, I turn to your loving embrace, entering the shrine of silence ~ SACRED SILENCE ~ I give you thanks as my soul is reconsecrated by your silence.

Soul-friends all, teacher of my soul, as the Autumn light ripens the grain and fruits of the earth, so I seek to ripen my soul with your help. Lead me along pathways where I can find answers to the question of this day ~ SOLAR QUESTION.

May all who carry heavy responsibilities be given the strength and commitment to fulfill their duties with lightness, humor and respect, especially . . . .
. . . . .

I give thanks for the fertility of the earth's harvest: there is more than enough to share with all. May the abundant gifts of the sweet earth be apportioned with generous hands to all beings in need.

I acknowledge the spiritual life and mystical commitment of other faiths, especially . . . . May all people of goodwill realize their common spiritual bond for the benefit of all beings in the universe. May no searching soul be excluded from the communion of the Divine Spirit.

I go forth today under the
Cloak of Covering:
triumph of treetops,
majesty of foliage,
lightness of leaves,
strength of trunk,
suppleness of bark,
power of branches,
stability of roots,
penetration of sap,
energy of growth.
May no harm befall me
under the covering of this forest cloak,
this day and this night.

May the blessing of the
Circler of Seasons,
the Encompasser of Life,
keep my soul safe this Autumn day.

MONDAY
e v e n i n g

Yeast of Life,
Ferment of Ecstasy,
I grow and ripen with you.
I return under the shade of twilight,
under the veils of work and worship.

Brightness breaks at twilight's falling,
candle quivers in the dark;
soul-freight bids heart's hopeful calling
bring soul-healing with its spark.

As the abundance of Autumn gathers its goodness on every side, I call upon my soul's teacher to reveal the sources of nourishment that this day has offered ~ SELF-CLARIFICATION ~ May the Mother of Life, the Father of Light, be merciful to all in need of body or soul.

I enter the sanctuary of stillness, O Keeper of the Heart-Shrine, there to be safe-kept in you ~ SACRED SILENCE ~ As the moon tracks its faithful path across the heavens, so I turn to you for the illumination of its mystery ~ LUNAR MEDITATION.

I give thanks to the trees and forests for their cloak of covering: may the sacred canopy of leaves continue to mantle the planet with its life-giving inspiration and protection. May the forests be preserved with loving respect.

May all who fear failure, may all who have to succeed or be consequently diminished, learn from the humility of making mistakes; may the Preserver of Promises bring them to the plateau of confident and unconditional surrender.

I ask a blessing upon all in poverty: may the Holy Ones shower the grace of abundant joy and security upon those in need.

For my dear ones and my dead ones, for my family and friends, I ask a blessing, especially for . . . .

I mantle my soul in the mercy of creation,
light of heaven above me,
life of earth about me,
love of ocean beneath me.
May the mercy of creation
surround and encompass all beings
from fall of night
till crack of light,
in the perfection of peace.

Sovereign of the Stars,
Compassionate Queen of the Night,
I enter the refuge of sleep.

99

TUESDAY
m o r n i n g

Sovereign of the Earth,
Compassionate Queen of the Planet
Keeper of the Universe,
In your mystery I arise.

I waken my soul with the
chimes of the silver branch:
note of gladness,
note of clearness,
note of devotion,
be within my heart, my mind, my soul.
May my soul be preserved
from day's dawning
till twilight's awning.

Abiding Presence of the Deep Worlds, while I have slept, you have been hastening Autumn. Before I enter the motion of the fruiting season, I rest in the stillness of your deep abiding ~ *SACRED SILENCE* ~. Though the sun circles farther from us, may I never be far from the warm embrace of your silent presence.

Soul-friends, soul-teacher, I call upon your guidance this day. I do not know what lies before me, but I ask your help now to consider clearly the issue of this day ~ *SOLAR QUESTION* ~ Accompany me throughout the mazes of this day, that I may be surely led.

May the Great Provider have mercy upon those who are starving: may the Holy Ones assist them, and may we all learn respect for the just apportioning of the world's food.

Emotional storms of life sweep into the lives of many like the equinoctial gales of Autumn; may the Keeper of the Winds' Compass help all in turmoil to find the still center of peaceful resolution especially . . . .

May all who are driven to the shelter of addictions begin to be aware of the safety of their true home: may the Holy Ones shower comfort and healing upon them that they may return from the exile of abuse into the temple of self-respect.

I mantle myself in the
covering of creatures:
stillness of owl,
perception of eagle,
humility of wren,
speed of horse,
strength of bear,
courtesy of deer,
repose of serpent,
silence of mouse,
courage of salmon.
Nine creatures about me
to clothe and protect me,
on the ways that I walk.

May the blessing of the Bright One,
Companion of Souls,
be upon me and upon all whom I love.

TUESDAY
e v e n i n g

Traveler of Inner Space,
Explorer of the Stars,
Discoverer of New Worlds,
my quest is made perfect in you.

Harvest fires, brightness burns,
harvest byres, Autumn turns,
candle flickering, soul discerns.

As the winds of Autumn dash the leaves from the trees, so I call upon my soul's teacher to help me gather up the many scattered fragments of this day ~ SELF-CLARIFICATION ~ May all the little victories of today overset the willful defeats in the scales of life.

Steward of the Universe, I turn once more to you. Into the treasury of my soul I commit the riches of this day, offering you . . . . Beloved of my heart, now in silence I enter the sanctuary where all souls meet ~SACRED SILENCE ~ Pledged in love to this dear life, I ask your help to consider the mystery of this night ~ LUNAR MEDITATION.

Bountiful Mother and Father, I ask a blessing upon all who gather in the harvest at this season. May each farm, orchard, and garden be blessed with abundance and may each be tended with respectful love.

May all who replay the trauma of past events be restored to the power and help of the present moment; may the Holy Ones lead them from the spirals of the mind's maze to the steady circuits of the sun, the moon and the stars.

Keeper of the Heart, kindle compassion in me when my heart threatens to close its doors. There are many for whom my heart's door shuts when I see or consider them; I take time now to breathe blessing upon them, especially . . . . I give thanks to the qualities of creatures that have been my mantle this day: may all their kind be blessed.

I quieten my soul with the
chimes of the silver branch:
great gladness in my heart,
no sadness in my mind,
rich rest within my soul.
May the three clear notes of the Soul-Keeper
resound through all beings,
bringing peace and rest
at this day's ending.

Vessel of Healing,
Cup of Transformation,
Ocean of Blessing,
I am but a drop of your draft as I sink down
to sleep.

101

WEDNESDAY
m o r n i n g

From the Vessel of Healing,
from the Grail of Grace,
from the Ocean of Abundance,
I rise replenished.

From the treasury of my soul I draw forth,
gem of light,
gem of life,
gem of love:
three precious gems
to preserve my soul
from light to darkness
on this Autumn day.

Shield of Souls, I place myself in your protective silence. May we meet heart to heart ~ SACRED SILENCE ~ To you I dedicate the unfolding acts of this day.

Creative teacher of my soul, I waken to new thresholds this Autumn day. Before I set forth, help me explore the question of today with the mellow rays of sun's encircling ~ SOLAR QUESTION.

May I be on guard against complacency today.

I rejoice and celebrate the happiness of this season which is life's rich gift: may all who are in sorrow and grieving find solace in the richness of Autumn's bounty.

I ask a blessing on all who face critical decisions today: may the Holy Ones shed the light of discernment and justice upon them, especially . . . .

May all who die today know the touch of the Soul Gatherer as their souls pass from this world to the Land of Promise: may all who are facing death be granted a space of preparation that the house of their soul be made ready.

In my heart, I hold my dear ones and ask a blessing upon them this day . . . .

I go forth under the mantle
of the deep ocean's mystery:
height of swell,
whiteness of foam,
depth of trough,
torrent of shoal,
eddy of current,
roar of wave,
flood of tide,
wash of ebb,
generosity of flow,
be about me in beauty
and protection this Autumn day.
May my soul be preserved in peace.

May the blessing of the
Arch of Heaven be over me,
may the blessing of the
Abyss of Earth be under me,
may I be safe-kept in your care.

WEDNESDAY
e v e n i n g

Gatherer of Harvest,
Gleaner of Souls,
I am brought into the sheaf of your
love this night.

Candle brightening,
flame's own flower,
harbinger of daylight's ebb;
light the pathway to the bower –
find the way to spirit's web.

As I take off my clothes to sleep, so I cast off the garment of today and ask my soul's teacher to show me how my soul may be cleansed of all hurt and stain as I sleep this night ~ SELF-CLARIFICATION ~ May the Holy Ones cleanse and sustain my soul this night.

Fountain of Brightness, I come to greet you in the courts of bliss, under the seal of silence ~ SACRED SILENCE ~ For your mercy and courtesy I give you great thanks. As I seek the illumination of your mystery, may I be blessed this night ~ LUNAR MEDITATION.

I give thanks to the powers of the mighty ocean for surrounding me in their mantle this day: may the dear ocean and all the life within it be preserved and respected as life's first home and as the pathway of water.

May the blessing of the bonding of soul between spiritual kindred be recognized in every place: I look into my own experience and acquaintance, acknowledging those who share my soul's likeness and resonance . . . .

I ask a blessing on those who are unable to receive, on all who must be the sole givers and never the receivers: may the Holy Ones grant them a glad heart that can open to the touch of blessing.

May the vision and insight of this season, the gifts of Autumn awaken within me and in those whom I now remember . . . .

Into the treasury of my soul I place
gem of brow's light,
gem of senses' life,
gem of heart's love.
The shining of the three precious gems,
preserve my soul of all beings
from Autumn's dark
till Autumn's day.

The Keeper of Concord,
the Shield of Courage,
be my defense this Autumn night.

THURSDAY
m o r n i n g

PRACTICE FOR EACH THURSDAY IN LUGHNASADH

Compassionate Mystery,
Awakener of Revelation,
as you have prophesied,
so do I arise from your concealment.

I brighten my soul with the colors of
Autumn:
hue of light,
hue of life,
hue of love,
color my mind, my body, my heart.
May my soul be preserved
from chill of dawn
till call of dark.

Mysterious Beauty, words cannot describe my gratitude for the coming of the light; only the silent truth of my heart speaks and listens for your light ~ SACRED SILENCE ~ May your presence be my beacon this day.

Keeper of my soul's progress, dear . . . . : you have encouraged my passage through life, yet still it does not run as steady as the sun's turning: reveal to me the track of this day's question ~ SOLAR QUESTION.

May the gift of giving well up in me so that generosity be no stranger to my heart: I ask for help from all my soul-friends that the deep draft of generosity may irrigate the channels of my life.

Shelter of Ages, I ask blessing upon refugees and those in detention centers, all people who seek a better life in a new land but who exist in the between places in disillusion and poverty: may they find their true home, a place in society and self-respect.

Ecstasy of Life, may your Holy Ones bestow the flame of ecstasy upon all inspirers that creativity may catch and toss the dull hearts of all who live without energy back into the dancing blaze of life.

I go forth under the
mantle of earth:
clarity of glaciers,
silence of deserts,
beauty of mountains,
sweetness of valleys,
mystery of forests,
flow of rivers,
depth of oceans,
equity of plains,
homeyness of hills.
Earth-mantle cover me,
keep and preserve me,
from strike of spark
till fall of dark.

Prophetic Utterance,
Sibyl of Silence,
I go forth with you.

THURSDAY
e v e n i n g

Prophetic Utterance,
Sibyl of Silence,
as a word of truth,
I return with you.

Heart's flame, bright fire, seal of night,
soul's lave, day's grave, trouble's flight,
now abides the living light.

As the birds go to roost at twilight, so I come to my soul's teacher to be shown how I can best put this day to bed ~ SELF-CLARIFICATION ~ May the troubles of today be soothed and rectified by the Holy Ones.

Divine Mother and Father, you are one with the world's wonder. As a child of wonder, I come into the shrine of the heart to greet you ~ SACRED SILENCE ~ In the silence of this Autumn evening, I give you thanks and ask your help to consider this night's mystery ~ LUNAR MEDITATION.

I give thanks for the gift of human vulnerability by which I am granted insight into the souls of others: I give thanks for the experiences that have opened doors in my separate nature, especially for the experience of . . . .

I ask a blessing on all whose lives are crippled by jealousy: may they be gifted with the freedom of a giving, generous heart that allows room for others and sets the soul free.

Laughter of the Ages, may your Holy Ones dispense the glad gift of divine humor that humanizes all grudging hearts and brings delight to the eyes.

I give thanks to the mantle of the earth that has wrapped me warmly this Autumn day; may the holy beauty of the earth be discerned in every one of its land-forms and features. May I ever tread softly upon you.

I veil my soul with the hues of Autumn:
veil of light upon my mind,
veil of life upon my body,
veil of love upon my heart.
The blessing veil of Autumn's dusk
be upon all beings,
both now and then,
both now and when.

Shrine of Souls,
Treasury of Hearts,
I take sleeping sanctuary in you.

Keeper of the Cauldron,
Alchemist of the Mystery,
I am remade in you.

I raise my soul from the kist of quietness,
beauty of love,
beauty of life,
beauty of light,
attend my heart, my body, my mind.
May my soul be preserved,
may it shed beauty on all beings
from dawn till dusk.

Keeper of the Cauldron, many elements of my life swirl about me in turmoil; may I enter your wholeness to savor their meaning in silence ~ SACRED SILENCE ~ I give thanks, for in you all elements are resolved.

Soul-teacher, weaver of my soul, send forth your shining ball of thread, that I may follow the track of this day's turning ~ SOLAR QUESTION.

May the world never lack wonder: the splendor of the rainbow, the magnitude of the oceans, the height of the mountains surround us on every side. May the Holy Ones preserve all shrines of natural wonder.

I ask a blessing upon all who hold the government of the world in their hands: may the Vigilant Judge and the Lady of Justice grant them purification of motives and responsibility of actions.

I am caught up in a whirlpool of events that leaves me little time to understand the meaning of my life: I ask my soul-friends for good judgment and discrimination in all I do, especially in the events that trouble me at this moment. . . . .

I go forth under the mantle
of the Autumn constellations:
power of Pegasus,
protection of Aries,
wonder of Cetus,
guidance of Piscus Australis,
abundance of Capricorn,
beauty of Andromeda,
alchemy of Aquarius,
justice of Triangulum,
transformation of Pisces.
Nine constellations
to cloak and cover me,
this day without fear.

Melody of Autumn,
Heart-beat of Harvest,
I set forth to your music this day.

FRIDAY
e v e n i n g

Queen of Homing,
King of Harvest, Sovereign of Souls,
I return to your courts this night.

Leaf-light: mantle of the night;
chief-light: diadem of sight;
soul-light: sovereign of heart's right.

Heavy with the burdens of this day, I call upon my soul's teacher to help me unburden the freight of today ~ *SELF-CLARIFICATION* ~ May the house of my soul be set in order.

I open the tired and empty spaces of my soul to your presence, Healer of Hearts. So fill me that I may rise with a store of courage and compassion ~ *SACRED SILENCE* ~ Generous Provider of plenty, I give you thanks for your restoring love; help me to unravel the mystery of the night ~ *LUNAR MEDITATION*.

I ask a blessing on all who direct the communication networks of the world: may they balance truth and responsibility, power and revelation that the soul of no being may be marred or misrepresented.

May the needs of all who lack medicine and proper health care be made known to you, Healer of Hearts, especially . . . .

I give thanks to the Autumn constellations for their starry protection; may their shining light mercifully shower a blessing upon all beings.

I offer the fruit and harvest of this week for the benefit of . . . .

May all whom I love be blessed, especially . . . .

I commit my soul into the kist of quietness,
my heart a casket of love,
my body a casket of life,
my mind a casket of light.
May the soul-shrine of all beings
be preserved in beauty
from dusk till dawn.

Healer of Hearts,
Solace of the Soul,
Into the womb of sleep I am sinking.

SATURDAY
m o r n i n g

Wakener of Hearts,
Inspirer of Souls,
I arise refreshed in you.

⊚

I kindle my soul in the embrace of
the Soul's Beloved:
touch of skill,
touch of craft,
touch of grace,
be upon my eyes, my hands, my heart.
May my soul be preserved in peace,
from dawn's own light,
till swift twilight.

Dancer of the Leaves, you have been hastening Autumn while I slept, and the trees grow barer. Shake the leaves of drowsiness from me now, so that I can enter your silent dance ~ SACRED SILENCE ~ I give thanks for the many gifts you have given me.

Teacher of my soul, you keep my faltering steps upon the path of spirit through your wonderful example. I especially appreciate your . . . . With the insight of your wisdom, please help me understand the question of this day ~ SOLAR QUESTION.

I ask a blessing on those who cannot conceive a child: may the blessing of kindred-hearts relieve the sorrow of the unconceiving, and may the Holy Ones grant them the power to parent in other, loving ways.

Temperer of Souls, grant assistance to all whose anger, panic or fear cause them to frequently lose control: I ask help also for myself especially when . . . .

I give thanks for all the gifts and abilities that I have received: help me to better appreciate my gift of . . . .

❬❬❬❬❬

I draw around my being
the cloak of covering,
glory of gardens,
fruit of orchards,
fertility of fields,
healing of herb-plots,
plenty of plantations,
nurture of nurseries,
wine of vineyards,
medley of meadows,
grace of grasslands.
The mantle of earth
be about my shoulders
this day and night,
this night and day.

❦

May the blessing of Radiant One,
the Brightener of Mornings
attend my steps this day.

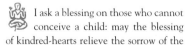

SATURDAY
e v e n i n g

> *Lyre of Delight,*
> *Harp of Harmony,*
> *Into your harmony I am woven.*

Breath of fire, burning flame,
blesséd is the gift you bear;
heart's sorrow, soul's claim,
cleansing gift of candle prayer.

Keeper of my soul's journey, I review my life to the present moment ~ *SELF-CLARIFICATION* ~ May the patterns of my life be clarified and rewoven into the garment of creation. Soul's teacher, may the inspiration of your guardianship lead me to fullness of life and potential.

Harmony of the Cosmos, in you the notes of every soul make one music. Calm the discord in my heart so that I may cross the threshold of peace ~ *SACRED SILENCE* ~ May this blessed music guide me on my spiritual path to my life's ending. As night falls and the birds cease their singing, so I turn to your mysterious cave of darkness; show to me the illumination of my quest ~ *LUNAR MEDITATION.*

I give thanks for the powers of the earth's bounty which have been my cloak of covering this day: may we respect the cycles of growth and the miracle of the food-chain without chemical interference or pollution.

I ask a blessing upon all women whose wombs are fertile with new life: may the Holy Ones assist those who welcome this new life, may they support all who are unable to give that welcome and receive all unborn souls in peace.

I celebrate the lives of all who have overcome great difficulties with grace and resourcefulness to live lives of inspirational courage, especially . . . .

I gather within the space of my heart all whom I love and yearn for . . . .

I rest my soul in the embrace of
the Soul's Beloved:
skill of eye,
craft of hand,
grace of heart,
be upon my soul and upon all beings.
May the embrace of the Beloved Spirit
preserve all souls in peace,
from swift twilight
till dawn's dear light.

Into the Womb of Night I am traveling,
into the Cavern of the Dark I am coming;
may the blessing of deep sleep attend me,
may the blessing of good dreams
accompany me.

SUNDAY
m o r n i n g

Miracle of Mornings,
Marvel of Mercy,
I come forth with you this morning.

I kindle my soul from the Autumn sunlight,
glow of life,
glow of light,
glow of love,
be upon my being, my heart and my soul
this Autumn day,
from break of light,
till fall of night.

Source of Rest, I seek the recreation of your deep silence, in the meeting place of peace ~ SACRED SILENCE ~ Cup of Blessing, you have filled my heart; may I brim with blessedness this day.

Soul-friends all, I call upon your playful spirit to help lighten my soul. As the Autumn sun tracks its way toward Winter, may I enjoy the questing and the questioning of this day ~ SOLAR QUESTION.

I ask a blessing on all who are seeking for justice, for all who suffer the law's delay: may the Holy Ones bring the gift of merciful justice to those who are innocent yet stand accused.

As the days shorten and the nights lengthen, may all who withdraw into the hermitage of the heart find spiritual refreshment and divine peace.

When my heart is empty of spirit, may the Holy Ones help rekindle it and lead me to find the special, personal ways that will help me keep it burning. I bring to mind the paths along which my heart already travels . . . .

I give thanks for the delight of my sexuality: may I respect my sexual needs within a greater respect for others with whom I share my love.

I take the cloak of covering
from the fruits of nine trees:
blessing of cherry,
richness of plum,
knowledge of apple,
melody of pear,
sweetness of peach,
brightness of orange,
ecstasy of grape,
sharpness of lemon,
fertility of fig.
Nine fruits and nine flavors
to preserve my soul
in peace this day.

May the blessing of the Messenger of Joy,
may the blessing of the Renewer of Hearts,
accompany me this Autumn day.

SUNDAY
e v e n i n g

Hostel of Harvest,
Welcomer at the Feast,
I am welcome within your walls.

Moon-beam, life-dream, candle shining,
star-gleam dancing in the night;
heart's scheme, soul's stream now combining,
burn unflickering, holy light.

As the Autumn gales dash themselves upon the coast, so I cast myself into the merciful arms of my soul's teacher. Give me understanding of this week's events, the breakthroughs and the revelations, the failures and the mistakes ~ SELF-CLARIFICATION ~ May the tides of change sweep away all that is outworn and strengthen whatever is eternal in my life.

Singer of Twilight, I am drawn once more into your melody. At the heart of the chorus is the stillness of your greeting ~ SACRED SILENCE ~ As Autumn turns to Winter, may I never lose this pathway to the Divine Heart. The sealing of the dark heralds the preparation for a new day; as the stars shine forth, reveal to me your mystery ~ LUNAR MEDITATION.

I give thanks to the friendship of fruits that have been my mantle this day: may your many flavors continue to delight us, may your many species never die out.

I ask a blessing on all who are contemplating partnership in business, creative effort or emotional life: may the Holy Ones grant them perfect harmony.

In the place of evening, I speak to my descendants – my blood-kin and my spiritual kindred alike – to you I leave the heritage of this season: . . . . (speak of the treasures of your season's experience that you would like to survive you, to help others.)

Wound in the beauty of this Autumn night, I hold in my heart those who are in need . . . .

I shield my soul as the Autumn moon rises:
glow of life shield my being,
glow of light shield my heart,
glow of love shield my soul,
this Autumn night.
May the soul of all beings be blessed
from fall of night,
till break of light.

Mother of Mercy,
Father of Faithfulness,
I sing your song of sleep.
May all beings find rest in the Courts of Joy.

Solar Questions for Lughnasadh

These questions are part of the morning devotion, to be asked and answered during that time, or to be considered during the day. Some of the answers may reveal aspects of yourself you had not considered, some may require practical implementation. Each day corresponds to the calendrical date, for example: on 14 September, you consult the question on Day 14 below.

~ 1 ~
What soul-food nourishes you?

~ 2 ~
What riches lie in your treasury?

~ 3 ~
Are you doing too much and which areas can be pruned?

~ 4 ~
Are you abusing or respecting other's boundaries?

~ 5 ~
What needs to be fulfilled or accomplished right now?

~ 6 ~
Where do you need to conserve your resources?

~ 7 ~
How do you use the world's resources to sustain your life?

~ 8 ~
What traditional frameworks support you?

~ 9 ~
What harmony is calling you to play?

~ 10 ~
Who needs to be gratefully acknowledged in your life?

~ 11 ~
What sorrow is unexpressed within you?

~ 12 ~
Where do you need to invest your trust at this time?

~ 13 ~
What is your spiritual goal?

~ 14 ~
What is transforming within you?

~ 15 ~
When did you last celebrate or party?

~ 16 ~
Do you practice hospitality of spirit?

~ 17 ~
Which of your skills needs to be honed at this time?

~ 18 ~
What joy do you miss most: where is joy within you?

~ 19 ~
What areas of your life need hard or steady work right now?

~ 20 ~
What motivates your lifestyle?

~ 21 ~
Do you overconsume the world's resources?

~ 22 ~
Are you appropriating someone else's resources or time?

~ 23 ~
How is truth served in your life?

~ 24 ~
Do you abuse or respect obligations?

~ 25 ~
What excites your soul?

~ 26 ~
What do you appreciate most about your skills?

~ 27 ~
Which old habits do you need to change?

~ 28 ~
Are you in touch with your emotions?

~ 29 ~
Which unacknowledged needs are eating holes in you?

~ 30 ~
Which ideas and structures have you outgrown?

~ 31 ~
What needs liberating in your life?

Lunar Meditations for Lughnasadh

The following meditation subjects may be selected for the appropriate phase of the moon each evening. See the perpetual moon calendar on p.116 for the correct phase.

~ 1 ~
The freedom of a decisive action you must take.

~ 2 ~
An absent friend.

~ 3 ~
The blessing of water.

~ 4 ~
A tree of your choice.

~ 5 ~
The lessons of illness.

~ 6 ~
The creative power of hope.

~ 7 ~
The urgency of vocation.

~ 8 ~
The courage to change.

~ 9 ~
The vista through the window.

~ 10 ~
The message of the blood.

~ 11 ~
The glory of the sunset.

~ 12 ~
The tides of moon and sea.

~ 13 ~
The song of the earth.

~ 14 ~
The silent accord of true love.

~ 15 ~
The harvest of your soul.

~ 16 ~
The alchemy of Autumn.

~ 17 ~
A song of your choice.

~ 18 ~
The grail of your search.

~ 19 ~
The tranquillity of gardens.

~ 20 ~
The freedom of letting go.

~ 21 ~
The restoration of sleep.

~ 22 ~
Memory of places distant or no more.

~ 23 ~
Sources of comfort.

~ 24 ~
The relief of problem's dissolution.

~ 25 ~
A poem of your choice.

~ 26 ~
The blessing of twilight.

~ 27 ~
The companionship of animals.

~ 28 ~
The nonexistence of time.

~ 29 ~
The dimensions of the universe.

Perpetual Lunar Calendar

THE PERPETUAL LUNAR CALENDAR was created by Madeleine Johnson, who also wrote the Moon Notes. The Calendar enables you to calculate the lunar phase for any given day, so that you can determine which of the lunar meditations are appropriate to your seasonal devotions.

Because this Calendar covers a repeating 19 year cycle, it is impossible to give exact correspondences of dates and lunar phases in tabular form, so only the four major Moon phases are indicated on the chart: the New, Waxing Quarter, Full and Waning Quarter phases. Each column of the Calendar shows these four phases in association with a number that is the date of the month on which these phases fall. The day of the New Moon, indicated on the Perpetual Lunar Calendar chart by a dark circle, is Day 1 of the lunar cycle.

EXAMPLE: To find the corresponding lunar phase for 29 September 1998 – read along the top line of the chart to find the current year. We find that 1998 is shown in column 3. Now read down the chart to find the current month: we find September is in the ninth column under 1998. The nearest Moon phase shown to the 29 is 28 September, which is a waxing quarter Moon, towards the end of the Moon cycle that began on the 20 September 1998. The beginning of that Moon cycle corresponds to the following lunar days:

KEY

New or "Dark" Moon

○
Full Moon

)
Waxing Quarter Moon
(the moon is waxing when you
can cup it in your right hand)

(
Waning Quarter Moon
(the moon is waning when you
can cup it in your left hand)

20 Sept 1998 = Day 1 or New Moon,
21 Sept = Day 2, *22 Sept* = Day 3,
23 Sept = Day 4, *24 Sept* = Day 5,
25 Sept = Day 6, *26 Sept* = Day 7,
27 Sept = Day 8, *28 Sept* = Day 9 or
Quarter Waxing Moon, *29 Sept* = Day 10 etc.

	1996/ 2015 1	1997/ 2016 2	1998/ 2017 3	1999/ 2018 4	2000/ 2019 5	2001/ 2020 6
Jan	○/5 ◑/13 ●/20 ◐/27	◑/2 ●/9 ◐/15 ○/23 ◑/31	◐/5 ○/12 ◑/20 ●/28	○/2 ◑/9 ●/17 ◐/24 ○/31	●/6 ◐/14 ○/21 ◑/28	◐/2 ○/9 ◑/16 ●/24
Feb	○/4 ◑/12 ●/18 ◐/26	●/7 ◐/14 ○/22	◐/3 ○/11 ◑/19 ●/26	◑/8 ●/16 ◐/23	●/5 ◐/12 ○/19 ◑/27	◐/1 ○/8 ◑/15 ●/23
Mar	○/5 ◑/12 ●/19 ◐/27	◑/2 ●/9 ◐/16 ○/24 ◑/31	◐/5 ○/13 ◑/21 ●/28	○/2 ◑/10 ●/17 ◐/24 ○/31	●/6 ◐/13 ○/20 ◑/28	◐/3 ○/9 ◑/16 ●/25
Apr	○/4 ◑/10 ●/17 ◐/25	●/7 ◐/14 ○/22 ◑/30	◐/3 ○/11 ◑/19 ●/26	◑/9 ●/16 ◐/22 ○/30	●/4 ◐/11 ○/18 ◑/26	◐/1 ○/8 ◑/15 ●/23 ◐/31
May	○/3 ◑/10 ●/17 ◐/25	●/6 ◐/14 ○/22 ◑/29	◐/3 ○/11 ◑/19 ●/25	◑/8 ●/15 ◐/22 ○/30	●/4 ◐/10 ○/18 ◑/26	○/7 ◑/15 ●/23 ◐/29
Jun	○/1 ◑/8 ●/16 ◐/24	●/5 ◐/13 ○/20 ◑/27	◐/2 ○/10 ◑/17 ●/24	◑/7 ●/13 ◐/20 ○/28	●/2 ◐/9 ○/16 ◑/25	○/6 ◑/14 ●/21 ◐/28
Jul	○/1 ◑/7 ●/15 ◐/23 ○/30	●/4 ◐/12 ○/20 ◑/26	◐/1 ○/9 ◑/16 ●/23 ◐/31	◑/6 ●/13 ◐/20 ○/28	●/1 ◐/8 ○/16 ◑/24 ●/31	○/5 ◑/13 ●/20 ◐/27
Aug	◑/6 ●/14 ◐/22 ○/28	●/3 ◐/11 ○/18 ◑/25	○/8 ◑/14 ●/22 ◐/30	◑/4 ●/11 ◐/19 ○/26	◐/7 ○/15 ◑/22 ●/29	○/4 ◑/12 ●/19 ◐/25
Sep	◑/4 ●/12 ◐/20 ○/27	●/1 ◐/10 ○/16 ◑/23	○/6 ◑/13 ●/20 ◐/28	◑/2 ●/9 ◐/17 ○/25	◐/5 ○/13 ◑/21 ●/27	○/2 ◑/10 ●/17 ◐/24
Oct	◑/4 ●/12 ◐/19 ○/26	●/1 ◐/9 ○/16 ◑/23 ●/31	○/5 ◑/12 ●/20 ◐/28	◑/2 ●/10 ◐/17 ○/24 ◑/31	◐/5 ○/13 ◑/20 ●/27	○/2 ◑/10 ●/16 ◐/24
Nov	◑/3 ●/11 ◐/18 ○/25	◐/7 ○/14 ◑/21 ●/30	○/4 ◑/11 ●/19 ◐/27	●/8 ◐/16 ○/23 ◑/29	◐/4 ○/11 ◑/18 ●/25	○/1 ◑/8 ●/15 ◐/22 ○/30
Dec	◑/3 ●/10 ◐/17 ○/24	◐/7 ○/14 ◑/21 ●/29	○/3 ◑/10 ●/18 ◐/26	●/7 ◐/16 ○/22 ◑/29	◐/4 ○/11 ◑/18 ●/25	◑/7 ●/14 ◐/22 ○/30

Phase of Moon/Date of Month e.g. ○/1 – Full Moon/1st

MOON NOTES

❖ The Moon has many cycles – the Phases of the Moon, the passage each month of the Moon through the 360 degrees of the zodiac, the 19 year cycle which sees the return of the Moon to a synchronizing of the phase with the day of the year, and so on. Moon cycles are interrelated with those of the Sun and the Earth, indeed its phases are not just about the Moon, they are a visual representation of the interrelationship between the Sun, the Earth and the Moon. Their relative positions are never exactly the same, so that all its cycles must be approximate.

	2002/ 2021	2003/ 2022	2004/ 2023	2005/ 2024	2006/ 2025	2007/ 2026	2008/ 2027
	7	8	9	10	11	12	13
Jan	(/6 ●/13 D/21 ○/28	●/2 D/10 ○/18 (/25	○/7 (/15 ●/21 D/29	(/3 ●/10 D/17○/25	D/6 ○/14 (/22 ●/29	○/3 (/11 ●/19 D/25	●/8 D/15 ○/22 (/30
Feb	(/4 ●/12 D/20 ○/27	●/1 D/9 ○/16 (/23	○/6 (/13 ●/20 D/28	(/2 ●/8 D/16 ○/24	D/5 ○/13 (/21 ●/28	○/2 (/10 ●/17 D/24	●/7 D/14 ○/21 (/29
Mar	(/6 ●/14 D/22 ○/28	●/3 D/11 ○/18 (/25	○/6 (/13 ●/20 D/28	(/3 ●/10 D/17 ○/25	D/6 ○/14 (/22 ●/29	○/3 (/12 ●/19 D/25	●/7 D/14 ○/21 (/29
Apr	(/4 ●/12 D/20 ○/27	●/1 D/9 ○/16 (/23	○/5 (/12 ●/19 D/27	(/2 ●/8 D/16 ○/24	D/5 ○/13 (/21 ●/27	○/2 (/10 ●/17 D/24	●/6 D/12 ○/20 (/28
May	(/4 ●/12 D/19 ○/26	●/1 D/9 ○/16 (/23 ●/31	○/4 (/11 ●/19 D/27	(/1 ●/8 D/16 ○/23 (/30	D/5 ○/13 (/20 ●/27	○/2 (/10 ●/16 D/23	●/5 D/12 ○/20 (/28
Jun	(/3 ●/10 D/18 ○/24	D/7 ○/14 (/21 ●/29	○/3 (/9 ●/17 D/25	●/6 D/15 ○/22 (/28	D/3 ○/11 (/18 ●/25	○/1 (/8 ●/15 D/22 ○/30	●/3 D/10 ○/18 (/26
Jul	(/2 ●/10 D/17 ○/24	D/7 ○/13 (/21 ●/29	○/2 (/9 ●/17 D/25 ○/31	●/6 D/14 ○/21 (/28	D/3 ○/11 (/17 ●/25	(/7 ●/14 D/22 ○/30	●/3 D/10 ○/18 (/25
Aug	(/1 ●/8 D/15 ○/22 (/31	D/5 ○/12 (/20 ●/27	(/7 ●/16 D/23 ○/30	●/5 D/13 ○/19 (/26	D/2 ○/9 (/16 ●/23 D/31	(/5 ●/12 D/20 ○/29	●/1 D/8 ○/16 (/23 ●/30
Sep	●/7 D/13 ○/21 (/29	D/3 ○/10 (/18 ●/26	(/6 ●/14 D/21 ○/28	●/3 D/11 ○/18 (/25	○/7 (/14 ●/22 D/30	(/4 ●/11 D/19 ○/26	D/7 ○/15 (/22 ●/29
Oct	●/6 D/13 ○/21 (/29	D/2 ○/10 (/18 ●/25	(/6 ●/14 D/20 ○/28	●/3 D/10 ○/17 (/25	○/7 (/14 ●/22 D/29	(/3 ●/11 D/19 ○/26	D/7 ○/14 (/21 ●/28
Nov	●/4 D/11 ○/20 (/27	D/1 ○/9 (/17 ●/23 D/30	(/5 ●/12 D/19 ○/26	●/2 D/12 ○/20 (/23	○/5 (/12 ●/20 D/28	(/1 ●/9 D/17 ○/24	D/6 ○/13 (/19 ●/27
Dec	●/4 D/11 ○/19 (/27	○/8 (/16 ●/23 D/30	(/5 ●/12 D/18 ○/26	●/1 D/8 ○/15 (/23 ●/31	○/5 (/12 ●/20 D/27	(/1 ●/9 D/17 ○/24 (/31	D/5 ○/12 (/19 ●/27

❖ The cycle known as the Phases of the Moon runs from one conjunction with the Sun to the next (New Moon to New Moon). This is also called a lunation by astrologers. The Moon's cycle is somewhat eccentric and does not fit neatly in with the Sun's daily and annual cycle, which is slightly out of synchronization with the Moon's! This period of New Moon to New Moon is called the synodic month, and even that isn't constant every month. The average synodic month for the Moon is 29 days, 12 hours, 44 minutes and 2.7 seconds, but it can vary by up to 13 hours.

❖ The tables here give the exact date – GMT time – for the first 19 years – 1996 to 2014. From 2015 onward although most of the dates are correct, they can be out from a few hours to a day or so either side, so if you feel the need to be exact, check a good daily newspaper for the daily phase of the Moon.

❖ For the purposes of this book, the tables show the four main phases of the Moon, Full; Waning Quarter (approximately 7 days later); New (also popularly known as "Dark" because this is the time of the month when the Moon is invisible), which is approximately 7 days later and directly opposite the Full Moon; and Waxing Quarter, again approximately another 7 days later. And so we return full cycle to the Full Moon.

	2009/ 2028 14	2010/ 2029 15	2011/ 2030 16	2012 2031 17	2013/ 2032 18	2014/ 2033 19
Jan	◐/4 ○/11 ◑/18 ●/30	◑/7 ●/15 ◐/23 ○/30	●/4 ◐/12 ○/19 ◑/26	◐/1 ○/9 ◑/16 ●/23 ◐/31	◑/5 ●/11 ◐/18 ○/27	●/1 ◐/8 ◑/24 ●/30
Feb	◐/2 ○/9 ◑/16 ●/25	◑/5 ●/14 ◐/22 ○/28	●/3 ◐/11 ○/18 ◑/24	○/7 ◑/14 ●/21	◑/3 ●/10 ◐/17 ○/25	◐/6 ○/14 ◑/22
Mar	◐/4 ○/11 ◑/18 ●/26	◑/7 ●/15 ◐/23 ○/30	●/4 ◐/12 ○/19 ◑/26	◐/1 ○/8 ◑/15 ●/22 ◐/30	◑/4 ●/11 ◐/19 ○/27	●/1 ◐/8 ○/16 ◑/24 ●/30
Apr	◐/2 ○/9 ◑/17 ●/25	◑/6 ●/14 ◐/21 ○/28	●/3 ◐/11 ○/18 ◑/25	○/6 ◑/13 ●/21 ◐/29	◑/3 ●/10 ◐/18 ○/25	◐/7 ○/15 ◑/22 ●/29
May	◐/1 ○/9 ◑/17 ●/24 ◐/31	◑/6 ●/14 ◐/20 ○/27	●/3 ◐/10 ○/17 ◑/24	○/6 ◑/12 ●/20 ◐/28	◑/2 ●/10 ◐/18 ○/25 ◑/31	◐/7 ○/14 ◑/21 ●/28
Jun	○/7 ◑/15 ●/22 ◐/29	◑/4 ●/12 ◐/19 ○/26	●/1 ◐/9 ○/15 ◑/23	○/4 ◑/11 ●/19 ◐/27	●/8 ◐/16 ○/23 ◑/30	◐/5 ○/13 ◑/19 ●/27
Jul	○/7 ◑/15 ●/22 ◐/28	◑/4 ●/11 ◐/18 ○/26	●/1 ◐/8 ○/15 ◑/23 ●/30	○/3 ◑/11 ●/19 ◐/26	●/8 ◐/16 ○/22 ◑/29	◐/5 ○/12 ◑/19 ●/26
Aug	○/6 ◑/13 ●/20 ◐/27	◑/3 ●/10 ◐/16 ○/24	◐/6 ○/13 ◑/21 ●/29	○/2 ◑/9 ●/17 ◐/24 ○/31	●/6 ◐/14 ○/21 ◑/28	◐/4 ○/10 ◑/17 ●/25
Sep	○/4 ◑/12 ●/18 ◐/26	◑/1 ●/8 ◐/15 ○/23	◐/4 ○/12 ◑/20 ●/27	◑/8 ●/16 ◐/22 ○/30	●/5 ◐/12 ○/19 ◑/27	◐/2 ○/9 ◑/16 ●/24
Oct	○/4 ◑/11 ●/18 ◐/26	◑/1 ●/7 ◐/14 ○/23 ◑/30	◐/4 ○/12 ◑/20 ●/26	◑/8 ●/15 ◐/22 ○/29	●/5 ◐/11 ○/18 ◑/26	◐/1 ○/8 ◑/15 ●/23 ◐/31
Nov	○/2 ◑/9 ●/16 ◐/24	●/6 ◐/13 ○/21 ◑/28	◐/2 ○/10 ◑/18 ●/25	◑/7 ●/13 ◐/20 ○/28	●/3 ◐/10 ○/17 ◑/25	○/6 ◑/14 ●/22 ◐/29
Dec	○/2 ◑/9 ●/16 ◐/24 ○/31	●/5 ◐/13 ○/21 ◑/28	◐/2 ○/10 ◑/18 ●/24	◑/6 ●/13 ◐/20 ○/28	●/3 ◐/9 ○/17 ◑/25	○/6 ◑/14 ●/22 ◐/28

The 29 lunar meditations can be used to fit into each monthly cycle of phases, using the table as a guide, and beginning with the New Moon as Phase 1, Waxing Quarter at Phase 8/9, Full Moon at Phase 14/15 , Waning Quarter at Phase 21/22 and returning to Phase 29/1 at the New Moon once more. Because of the eccentric nature of the Moon's cycles, you may find that you will not always need all 29 phases, and at other times there will be more than 29 days in the cycle. But the period of the dark and full Moons are so powerful that they can appear to last longer than just one day, so it can feel right to concentrate on and meditate on these phases for two or three nights. Your own intuition will guide you.

❖ Of course if you are not sure, you can always go out and look up into the sky. But you may not see anything even if the stars are bright and the sky is clear. Remember that the Full Moon always rises at Sunset, the New (Dark) Moon always rises at Sunrise, the Waning Quarter rises at Midnight and the Waxing Quarter rises at Noon. Each day the Moon rises around 50 minutes later. So you will see a waxing Moon in the evenings, but to view the waning Moon in the night sky you must be awake in the early morning, before Sunrise. If the day is clear you will still see its faint outline crossing the sky from east to west.

THE HOUSE OF LIFE

T HIS SECTION contains a selection of prayers, blessings and
practices for special occasions. There is a blank page for you
to record your own personal devotions.

BLESSING OF THE ELEMENTS
(to be said on using any of the elements in daily life)

Blessed be the precious and preserving air,
the breath of life, our inspiration and delight.
Blessed be the precious and preserving fire,
the blood of life, our warming guest.
Blessed be the precious and preserving water,
the water of life, our cleansing guest.
Blessed be the precious and preserving earth,
the flesh of life, our sustainer and our wisdom.

BLESSING OF THE NINE ELEMENTS FOR ALL OCCASIONS

May you go forth under the strength of heaven,
under the light of sun,
under the radiance of moon;

may you go forth with the splendor of fire,
with the speed of lightning,
with the swiftness of wind;

may you go forth supported by the depth of sea,
by the stability of earth,
by the firmness of rock;

may you be surrounded and encircled,
above, below and about,
with the protection of the nine elements.

KYTHING FOR ONE FAR DISTANT OR ABSENT

"To kythe" means "to be in the physical presence of" someone. This invocation
can therefore be useful to partners who wish to be in spiritual communion with
each other at a specific time during a planned absence.

Holy Ones, Messengers of Love,

I am parted from . . . . ;

take my love and blessing to her/him wherever s/he is at this moment.

May s/he feel the warmth of my presence as I bring

her/him into the circle of my heart at this time~

SILENT COMMUNION WITH THE ABSENT ONE.

May you walk in the presence of the Holy Ones in every place,

may the Friend of Souls be ever at your side,

and may you be blessed and protected wherever you go!

BLESSING FOR LOVED ONES WANDERING IN UNKNOWN PLACES

The blessing of my love be ever with you,

Over sea, over shore, over stone.

PRAYER IN URGENT NEED

(In the grip of need, there are often no adequate
words: let the urgency of your need speed to the
sources of help with:)

O Greatness, hear!

O Brightness, hark!

Leave us not little, nor yet dark!

BLESSING FOR A FAMILY GATHERING

May the hearth be gladdened
by the laughter of children,
by the kinship of clan,
by the wisdom of elders,
by the memory of souls passing,
by the joy of souls yet to be born.
No word or thought to darken the day,
No remembrance or sorrow to trammel the night.
But sun, moon and stars to brighten the gathering,
Songs, smiles and stories to share their delight.

BLESSING ON GIVING A GIFT TO SOMEONE

Take, and welcome joy within you:
Showers, flowers, powers,
Hatfulls, capfulls, lapfulls,
Treasures, measures, pleasures,
All be yours to enjoy!

BLESSING FOR A BRIDE & GROOM

Length of life and sunny days,
and may your souls not go homeward
till your own child falls in love!

BLESSING OF A NEW-BORN CHILD

(This formal blessing can be performed by the parents as they bathe the baby
in clean, warm water. Alternatively, a spontaneous blessing of different
qualities can be bestowed by a gathering of friends and family, each of whom
wishes the new-born child some good thing.)

A small wave for your form,
A small wave for your voice,
A small wave for your speech,
A small wave for your means,
A small wave for your generosity,
A small wave for your wealth,
A small wave for your life,
A small wave for your health.
Nine waves of grace upon you,
Waves of the Giver of Health.

BLESSING FOR THE SOUL'S RELEASE

You go home this night to your home of Winter,
To your home of Autumn, of Spring and of Summer;
You go home this night to your lasting home,
To your eternal bed, to your sound sleeping.

Sleep now, sleep, and so fade sorrow,
Sleep now, sleep, and so fade sorrow,
Sleep now, sleep, and so fade sorrow,
Sleep, my beloved, in the rock of the fold.

The sleep of seven lights upon you, my dear,
The sleep of seven joys upon you, my dear,
The sleep of seven slumbers upon you, my dear.

Sleep, oh sleep in the quiet of quietness,
Sleep, oh sleep in the way of guidance,
Sleep, oh sleep in the love of all loving.

SOUL-LEADING FOR SOMEONE
WHO HAS DIED
SUDDENLY OR UNEXPECTEDLY

You have been called from the place of your dwelling,
After times, after duties, after separations.
May blessed soul-friends guide you,
May helping spirits lead you,
May the Gatherer of Souls call you,
May the homeward path rise up under your feet
And lead you gladly home.

BLESSING FOR ANYONE
GOING INTO A DIFFICULT OR
DANGEROUS ENTERPRISE

May the Seeder of Quests direct your steps!
May the Holy Ones protect your passage!
May helping hands be extended to you on every side!

BLESSING FOR A STUDENT

May you be blessed by the nine gifts of the cauldron:
may the poetry of imagination be kindled in you,
may the insight of your reflections ripen the fruits of your meditation,
may you learn from the lore of the land,
may your research empower your descendants,
through the great knowledge of your ancestors,
may the sparkle of intelligence irradiate your life,
may understanding rest in your heart,
may wisdom reside in the depths of your soul.

BLESSING FOR GOOD DREAMS

On my right side I me lay
Blessed Lady to you I pray:
For the blessings that you set
On your people without let,
Grant me grace for to sleep
And good dreams for to meet.
Sleeping, waking till morrow day be,
O Lord the fruit, O Lady the tree,
Blessed the blossom that springs from thee.

PRAYER FOR SLEEPLESS NIGHTS

My heart has been turned from home, for I am wakeful.
As the desert hours stretch out to the stars,
As an exile banned from the native land of sleep,
I offer this prayer for all who are wakeful and alone.
In torment and danger, in fear and in despair,
In grief and watchfulness, in worry or in care,
May the Thatcher of Sleep make a roof for the wakeful soul,
May the Weaver of Dreams lend a garment to cover the wakeful,
May the Womb of Night become a cradle of rest for the restless.
May the exile be restored to the house of sleep.

BLESSING ON ANY VISION OR INSIGHT

O Brightness of brightness, o clearness of clear!
Aisling* of vision in my heart appear.
Blessed your fragrance, your grace is the dew
That on my soul falling shall heal me anew.

*Aisling (pronounced esh-ling) is a Gaelic term for a vision

PRAYER OF FORGIVENESS

Healer of Hearts, Counselor of Souls,
Each morning the miracle of life is renewed in me;
As I have been restored, time after time,
So now do I pass on the merciful gift to ......
On my part, I release him/her/them from any bond of anger, blame,
recrimination.
May all corrosive links between us be dissolved
By the blessed balm of peace and concord.

SOUL-GATHERING PRAYER AFTER A SUDDEN SHOCK

Gatherer of Souls, draw to me my scattered soul,
May no part be lost,
May no part be straying.
Preserve my soul in peace
In the soul-shrine of my body.

PRAYER FOR COURAGE TO
RE-ENCOUNTER SITUATIONS, PLACES OR PEOPLE
WHICH HAVE SHAKEN CONFIDENCE

I will rise, I will go back
To the white and silver shore.
I will have courage,
As the sun does rising and setting.
At birth and death, the gift of life is precious,
Soul-life streaming down the strand.
I will go as the sea in its turning,
I will rise, I will go back,
I will rise.

Your Devotions